KU-209-441

CHECKED   JUN 2008

Rec	
Stock no.	1cS07
Class	746
	AER
Labels √	
T √	

1037
746
AER

SILK BROCADES

India Crest

SILK BROCADES

YASHODHARA AGRAWAL

Lustre Press
Roli Books

All rights are reserved. No part of
this publication may be transmitted
or reproduced in any form or by
any means without prior permission
from the publisher.

ISBN: 81-7436-258-4

Second impression 2004
© **Roli & Janssen BV 2003**
Published in India by
Roli Books in arrangement
with Roli & Janssen BV
M-75, G. K. II Market
New Delhi-110 048, India.
Ph: ++91-11-29212271, 29212782
Fax: ++91-11-29217185
Email: roli@vsnl.com
Website: rolibooks.com

Design: Sneha Pamneja

Printed and bound in Singapore

CONTENTS

DEDICATION

~

Dedicated to that unknown spirit which is always there to guide me through the dark tunnel.

ACKNOWLEDGEMENTS

~

I am indebted to the weavers and designers of Varanasi whose in-depth knowledge of their craft has been a great source of inspiration. I particularly thank Shri Mukhtar Hussain, Shri Abu Sardar, Mohd.Yaseen, Shri Rakesh Singh, Prof Mohd. Toha, Shri Abdul Awwal, Shri Azizurrahman, Mohd. Nasir, Gani Baba, and Shri Sribhas Supkar for sharing their knowledge with me.

The help and co-operation I got from the late Ms Krishna Riboud, Ms Marie Helene Guelton (AEDTA, Paris), Ms Anamika Pathak (National Museum, New Delhi) cannot be expressed in words. Prof Shameem Akhtar, Head of Department, Persian language, Banaras Hindu University, was very generous whenever I needed her help in translating Persian words. I deeply thank Mr David de Souza (Mumbai) for photographing some textiles on my request beyond his scheduled time just to help me. My friend Ms Elsa Legitimo (Zurich) did the required French translation in the same spirit for which I am grateful. I wish to thank Dr T.K. Biswas, Joint Director, Bharat Kala Bhavan, Banaras Hindu University, for his co-operation. I thank Shri R.C. Singh and Shri P. Prakash Rao, photographers, Bharat Kala Bhavan.

Some information has been taken in this book from my Ph.D. work, submitted in Banaras Hindu University, Varanasi.

The help and support of the family cannot be expressed in words. Nevertheless, I would like to thank my uncle Shri Narayana Das (retired judge and ex-secretary to the Government of Uttar Pradesh and a writer in his own right) for going through the manuscript—an uphill task. My mother Mrs Nirmala Ramkrishna, my sisters Mrs Aruna Singh and Mrs Indu Agrawal, and my father the late Shri Ramkrishna (a scholar and writer himself) for having faith in me.

The author and the publisher thank Bharat Kala Bhavan, Varanasi; National Museum, New Delhi; Association pour l'étude et la documentation des textiles d'Asie, Paris; Victoria and Albert Museum, London; and private collectors for the illustrations they have provided.

INTRODUCTION

Textiles have fascinated mankind since ancient times. Many highly developed civilisations, besides their other achievements, produced incredibly refined and elaborately designed textiles – each created its own distinctive patterns, employed unique techniques, and utilised the raw materials available in the region, which were hemp, cotton, wool or silk.

It is regrettable, that in spite of the vast production of a diverse range of textiles over the centuries by civilisations renowned for the excellence of their textiles, Indian, Hellenic, Egyptian, Mesopotamian, Achaemidian, Sassanian, Assyrian and Chinese, only a minuscule fraction of fabric samples have survived the depredation of time due to their fragility.

Fragments of ancient fabrics in museums worldwide have been of invaluable help in discovering and understanding the historical background of textiles. Fabric found in Egyptian tombs, cotton fragments of the Indus Valley Civilisation excavated at Mohenjodaro, and silk and linen found in Central Asia at Chinese Turkestan sites (along the silk route) by Sir Aurel Stein throw a flood of light on the processes by which man created a multifarious range of exquisitely designed textiles.

Both India and China produced silk of two kinds: domesticated and undomesticated (which was also referred to as wild silk). In China sericulture was a highly organised industry under royal supervision, while in India it was mostly in the hands of the tribals of the area. Though India's speciality has traditionally been cotton, it was also known for its fine linen and silk fabrics. That silk fabrics were made in India in ancient times is corroborated by textual references in Indian literature. Ancient Indian texts refer to silk as *kausheya, kriminag, kitsutram, pattasutra* or *pattron* etc. These were varieties of wild silk, such as *tussar, eri* or *munga*, which were produced in particular parts of India such as Assam, upper Bengal, Madhya Pradesh and Orissa. This silk was obtained from the cocoon, without killing the worm, i.e., the silk was collected after the worm had left the cocoon. Hence, it was considered fit to be used for Hindu religious ceremonies and was also worn on special occasions by Buddhist monks who otherwise preferred cotton. However, Indian silk was considered inferior in quality to Chinese silk – Hiuen Tsang, the Chinese traveller in the seventh century, referred to it as 'wild silk'.

Till the second century A.D., China was the only producer of fine mulberry silk. The introduction of sericulture in Khotan and other Central Asian countries along the silk route (a name coined by Baron Ferdinand von Richtafen in the nineteenth century) ushered in a new era in the history of silk production. The inhabitants of Central Asia and other countries on the silk route benefitted the most from the silk trade, and people living in oases, as well as the nomadic tribes, were 'the earliest agents who transported silk products and transferred the technology of silk weaving and sericulture' (*Silk and*

Religion, Xinru Liu, p. 19). Though Chinese silk was still considered the best, it began to face stiff competition from the silk produced in these countries.

Chinese silk was introduced to India by traders (mainly from Samarkand and Bukhara), and it gained immense popularity among the royalty and the aristocracy. These fabrics and yarn were exported to the West via the regular trade routes by Indian traders, both by land and sea. Ancient Chinese texts mention a place named Huangche, which has been identified by scholars as Kanchi in south India – a silk brocade-weaving and trade centre. The expertise of Indian dyers in the art of dyeing fabrics in permanent luminous colours, also might have encouraged this trade via India.

The terms *hiranya drapi* (golden drape), *hiranya chandataka* (golden skirt), or *hiranya pesas* (gold embroidered), mentioned in ancient Indian texts, the *Rigveda* and the *Atharvaveda Samhita,* are the earliest references to Indian gold brocade. These gold and silver brocades (referred to later as *kamkhwab* or *kinkhab)* may have been similar to ancient fabrics such as *stavaraka* or *debag,* described as rich material of Persian origin, woven with silver and gold thread. The sun god, Surya, is described in early literature as being clad in a coat of *stavaraka.* A fabric such as this is also mentioned by Banbhatta, the seventh century scholar in the court of King Harsh Vardhana of Kanauj. He refers to it as *tarmukta stavaraka,* a brocade decorated with a border of pearls. He also mentions the *hansa* (swan or goose)-patterned material called *hansa dukula,* a fabric used by the gods and kings. Some linen and cotton fabrics were at par with silk, such as *dukul, kshauma, netra* and *tiritpatta.*

The Indian psyche was greatly influenced by nature's resplendent beauty – the sun, moon, stars, rivers, trees, flowers and birds. Subsequently, these images were ascribed meanings or used as references for the elaborately developed religious and spiritual themes in India's three major religions – Hinduism, Buddhism and Jainism. These classical motifs were incorporated in all art forms. A symbol-specific study, focusing on any particular motif, would yield a rewarding meaning – of interconnection and co-relation between its form and use in paintings, architectural carvings, textile designs, ceramics, metallurgy, jewellery, tile patterns, armament decorations, and so on. These religio-spiritual traditions, while divergent, developed side by side over many centuries, and therefore mutually influenced each others' usage of symbolism.

A study of the motifs found on the pottery of the Harappa civilisation reveals that certain motifs were common to a vast region, including India, Iran, Iraq, Afghanistan and Egypt, right up to parts of the Greek islands. (This is further corroborated by archaeological findings of sculpture, terracotta figurines and textile fragments.) The study reveals the amazing persistence of certain motifs over a period of three or four thousand years. The existence of figural and geometrical motifs such as trees, creepers, lotus flowers, bulls, horses, lions, elephants, peacocks, swans, eagles, the sun, stars, diagonal or zigzag lines, squares, roundels, and so forth, can be traced through the entire span of Indian art. Some became the speciality of a certain region or centre. These motifs occurred in almost every form of decorative art, including textiles.

Silk-weaving centres in India developed in and around the capitals of kingdoms, holy cities or trade centres. Well known silk brocade weaving centres were in Assam, Gujarat, Malwa and south

India and the migratory nature of the weavers helped in the development and creation of many new centres. Natural calamities, political or social reasons, a fall in patronage or non-availability of raw materials, usually drove them away in search of new centres. For example, many Gujarati weavers migrated to centres such as Tanjore, Trichinapally, Burhanpur, Chanderi and Varanasi due to repeated famine in their state. The centres developed in the north were Delhi, Agra, Fatehpur Sikri, Lahore, Kannauz, Mau, Azamgarh, Murshidabad and Varanasi. Though Varanasi was an ancient weaving centre for fine cotton and linen fabrics, silk weaving in its present form was introduced here much later, may be around the late seventeenth century.

Some of the finest textiles were made in the royal workshops, references to which have been found since the Mauryan period, third to first century B.C. This tradition was followed by later Indian kings including the Muslim rulers of the medieval period. Besides India weavers from the renowned brocade weaving centres of Persia and central Asia, such as Yezd, Susa, Ur, Khotan, Bukhara, Samarkand and Kashgar were employed in their royal workshops to make special fabrics for the royalty. According to the fourteenth century Arab traveller, Ibn Batuta (in *Rehla*), four thousand *khazzaz* (silk weavers) were employed in the atelier of the Delhi Sultan, Mohammad Tughlaq who made fabrics for royal needs. The techniques and designs introduced by them influenced the Indian weavers as well. They were also influenced by the trade in foreign brocades conducted through the ports of Surat and Bharuch in western India, evident particularly in the Gujarati brocades.

Rich materials were the exclusive prerogative of the crème de la crème of society, the rich and powerful merchants and noblemen, who not only could afford them but could even commission weavers to make fabrics for them. Particularly after the disintegration of the Mughal Empire many weavers worked for such new patrons. Religious functionaries too used these rich fabrics for their decorations and rituals. Well known south Indian temples had their own weavers to make materials exclusively for temple use.

An increasing demand for Indian textiles in European markets brought the Dutch, Portuguese, British and French traders to India in the seventeenth century. The weaving centres had to step up their production, to cater to the requirements of a much larger international market. The establishment of foreign trading companies in India during this period resulted in a tremendous boom in the variety and quality of textiles produced in the country. While the bulk of the material exported was cotton fabric, there was an overwhelming demand for other textiles too. The weaving centres met the challenge successfully. This was not only because of their long-standing weaving tradition, but also due to the weavers' familiarity with a wide range of materials and techniques. Diverse markets, changing tastes, contemporary fashions – all these factors infused new life into and greatly enhanced the quality of Indian silk brocades, which became world famous.

HISTORICAL PERSPECTIVE

The weaving of brocade was probably introduced in India by the Aryans, as spinning and weaving were important aspects of Aryan culture – they wove and made garments of wool and tree bark. According to Dr Motichandra, linen brocade and wool were popular with the Aryans because of the climatic conditions of the region they came from.

Excavations at Nevasa (in Maharashtra), however, proved that the use of silk was known to Indians in the fifteenth century B.C. In Vedic literature, terms such as *varasi, durshya, kshauma, panduvanik* and *tarpya* appear, which may refer to either linen or silk. *Tarpya* was a fabric of fine quality, used for sacrificial and other ceremonies. In the *Atharvaveda* it is said that city people wear clothes made of *tarpya*.[1]

Hiranya drapi,[2] *hiranya chandataka,*[3] *hiranya pesas,*[4] *hiranyakaship,* and other fabrics mentioned in Vedic literature, may have been textiles which were either embroidered or woven with gold. According to the *Rigveda, drapi*[5] was the upper garment or *uttariya*. Sayan, the fourteenth century Vedic scholar, describes *Pesas* as an ornament, but it was also used for gold-thread embroidery.[6] *Chandataka* was a short skirt-like garment, worn by both men and women, and the *hiranya chandataka* mentioned in the *Shatapatha Brahmana* was a gold-embroidered skirt worn by dancing girls.[7] *Hiranyakaship* was a golden pillow or bed.[8]

Patanjali, the celebrated grammarian of the second century B.C., mentioned a beautiful material called *shataka*[9] (which may have been used for an upper garment similar to an *uttariya,* worn by men) and also *shati,*[10] from which the word 'sari' has originated. These were made in Mathura, which had a large population of weavers. Its situation on the trade route and the easy availability of raw material may have been factors in the development of Mathura into an important silk-weaving centre.

Silk weaving was mentioned in Indian texts as early as in the third century B.C. The terms *kausheya, kriminag, kitsutram, pattasutra* or *pattron* perhaps referred to wild silk varieties[11] obtained from silkworms in the forests of Assam, West Bengal, Orissa, North India and Madhya Pradesh. The silkworm cocoons were collected by the local tribals – the Santhals, Kols, Khonds, Gondas or Pondraks.[12]

There are many varieties of undomesticated silkworms reared on different trees. Therefore, the quality, colour and names of the different kinds of silk vary accordingly. Maybe the word *kausheya,* used by Panini, was a general term for this category of silk. One variety was referred to

as *kusa* in the *Shatapatha Brahmana* (v. 2.1.8). Sayan also interpreted *kusa* as silk. Vedic literature mentions that during the *yajna* ceremony women wore *chandatakas* made of *kusa*. This may have been a wild silk obtained from a silkworm called *kuswari* or *kuswara,* reared on the *ber* (*zizyphus jujuba*) tree. *Kusa* was popular till the late nineteenth century in Lucknow, Banda, Hamirpur, Rae Bareilli, Unnao, and adjoining areas. It was also called *kosa* silk or Bhagalpur silk.[13]

Kosh and *kausheya* are mentioned in Sanskrit texts such as the *Shatapatha Brahmana,* Panini's *Sutrapat* and *Gunapat, Vashishta Dharmasutra* (11,66), *Vishnu Dharmasutra* (44,26), *Vaikhanas Dharmasutra* (3,4,2 *Pravar Khand*), *Shushruta Samhitas,* Kautilya's *Arthashashtra,* and later by the Sanskrit poet Kalidas and Banbhatta in their works. Panini[14] described *kausheya* as silk produced from *kosa* (cocoon), which perhaps referred to silk yarn found inside the cocoon. Later Katyayana, the ancient grammarian of the fourth century B.C., defined *kausheya* specifically as *vikar,* a product of *kos* (*vikara koshdyam*), i.e. silk fabric.[15] Patanjali too took the same view.

Mention is made of *kausheya* in both the great epics of India, the *Ramayana* and the *Mahabharata*. According to the Valmiki *Ramayana* (*Balkand* 74.4), Janak gave a large range of fabrics as dowry to his four daughters – they included cotton, silk, and *kshauma,* which was precious like silk. Another reference to *kausheya* is in the *Ayodhyakand* (37.9), where Sita is described as *kausheya vasini,* or the one who always wears silk garments. *Kausheya* is referred to in the *Mahabharata* in the *Sabha Parva*. In the

rajsuya yajna of King Yudhishtir, the king of Kamboj presented him with silk textiles from Bahlika (Balkh) and China, which did not have 'even a touch of cotton in them' (*Sabha Parva* 51.26), which meant that they were made of silk or *zari* (woven with gold or silver thread) and that mixed fabrics were also in use, which were cheaper than pure silk. Silk fabrics from the 'northern countries', decorated with silken pompoms, are also mentioned – these may have come from Central Asia.

Greek writers such as Strabo and Megasthenes[16] describe that gold-worked or woven garments were favoured by Indians, particularly on festive occasions during the reign of the Nandas (second century B.C.) and the Mauryas (fourth to second centuries B.C.). Of a ceremonial procession, Strabo[17] (the Greek writer of the first century B.C.) mentions that not only were the elephants adorned with gold and silver, but the attendants also wore garments embroidered and interwoven with gold.

During the Mauryan period, Madura, Aparanta, Kalinga and Kashi were the weaving centres for cotton fabric such as *madhu, aparantaka, kalingak, kashik,* and so forth. Though it is not clearly specified whether the fabrics were silk or brocade, it is clearly mentioned that the material was woven in the royal workshops under the supervision of a superintendent of weaving.[18] There is a possibility that silk textiles were woven in these centres, as the *pattron, kashik, paudrak* and *chinapatta* types of silk were available during that period.[19] These areas are still known for their silk fabrics. *Magadhika* and *paudrika* were

Preceding page 12

■ Plate: 2
BORDER FRAGMENT, PAITHAN/CHANDERI, 18TH CENTURY. SUCH LIGHT BROCADES IN TAPESTRY WEAVE MIGHT BE A CONTINUATION OF THE ANCIENT MANDASOR (MALWA) WEAVING. SUCH BROCADES WERE TUCKED IN *PATKAS* OR SARIS; THE WHITE *SOSAN* FLOWER HINTS AT A MUGHAL INFLUENCE.

varieties of *pattron* silk, made at Champa or Bhagalpur and in the ancient Pundra region (surrounded by Bengal, Orissa and Assam).

A variety of silk fabrics were woven between the first and third centuries A.D. In the *Divyavadan,* (the collection of Buddhist stories of the fourth century A.D.) words such as *pattanshuka, chinashuka, kausheya, dhautapatta, kashikanshuka, kashi,* and so forth, are mentioned. At that time Kashi or Varanasi (Banaras) was known for its fine cotton textile – there is no mention of its being a silk-manufacturing centre.[20] The meaning of *kashi* in the Sanskrit dictionary is shining or bright.[21] Therefore, shiny material with gold or silver decorations was probably called *kashikanshu* or *kashi.*[22] Usually fabrics were named after their place of manufacture. Scholars like Dr Motichandra are of the view that Kashi was known for its cotton fabrics, and silk weaving was a later innovation. Another group of scholars believes that there existed a silk-weaving industry in ancient Kashi, and the material woven was called *kashika* or *kashikanshuka.* However, in the absence of any conclusive evidence, it can also be presumed that the so-called silk fabric of Kashi may have actually come from Kashgar[23] in Central Asia which was also mentioned as Kashi (on maps of the Silk Route). Kashgar was a well-known silk weaving and trading centre and an important Buddhist city with beautiful monasteries decorated with fine silk fabrics.

In the literature of the Gupta period (fourth to sixth centuries A.D.), *dukula* (particularly with the swan pattern) is described as perhaps the finest fabric. In the Kalidas poem of this time, *Kumarsambhava* (5,67), a disguised Shiva tries to dissuade Parvati from marrying him by comparing their attires. He asks Parvati, how she who is used to wearing swan-patterned *hansa dukula* can marry Shiva, who is always clad in elephant skin. Later Shiva transforms his elephant skin into *dukula,* the borders decorated with pairs of swans, referred to as *hansa mithuna. Dukula* is also mentioned by Kalidas in the *Vikramorvasiyam* (Part V) and in the *Ritusamhara* – it is referred to as silk, meant for autumn wear. *Chinanshuka* is referred to in the *Kumarsambhava* (7.3), and it is probable that during the fifth to sixth centuries A.D. there was an abundant flow of Chinese silk into India.

Banbhatta, in the *Harshacharita* (the biography of King Harsha Vardhana of Kanauj), mentions a variety of textiles and garments made of *kshauma* (linen), *badara* (cotton), *dukula* (bark silk), *amshuka* (muslin), and *netra* (shot silk), which were displayed on the occasion of the King's sister, Princess Rajyashri's marriage. He also refers to garments made of *lalatantu,* which was probably woven with thread made from the guts of silkworms.[24] He describes the King wearing a *hansa dukula* garment during the ceremony of his accession to the throne. According to Banbhatta, Pundra Desh (Bengal) was the home of *dukula* and *kshauma* fabrics. The *Harshacharita* also mentions *pulakabandha, pushpapatta* and *chitrapatta. Pulakabandha* has been indentified by Dr Motichandra as a gaily coloured tie-and-dye fabric,[25] and *pushpapatta* as flowered silk.[26]

Facing page

■ Plate: 4
ODHNI, VARANASI, EARLY
20TH CENTURY. A *SATRANGI*
OR SEVEN-COLOURED
PATTERN INSPIRED BY THE
RAINBOW. THE USE OF
SEVERAL HUES ON A
GARMENT IS KNOWN
LOCALLY AS *CHATAPATI*. THE
ODHNI WELL ILLUSTRATES
THE *RANGKAT* TECHNIQUE.

Below

■ Plate: 3
A STRIPED *SATRANGI* FABRIC,
19TH CENTURY, VARANASI.

In *Kadambari*, Banbhatta describes the upper garment of Prince Chandrapid as *Indrayudhajalamber*. At one place, the multi-hued *uttariya* (upper garment) is described as *Indrayudhajalvarnanshukottariya*.[27] The pattern had different coloured stripes, or net designs called *jal* in a later period (Plates 3, 4). Such fabrics are seen in the cave paintings of Ajanta, but it is difficult to conclude whether the patterns were woven, or were tie-and-dye textiles. According to Dr V.S. Agrawal, complicated floral patterns, with many turns and twists, were developed in the Gupta period. They were called *atikutilpatralataprakarbhangur*, and were also used as decorative motifs in other branches of arts.[28]

From a passage in Shantideva's *Sikshasamuchchaya* (seventh century A.D.), we learn that Varanasi still retained its ancient reputation as the producer of the best silk. This perhaps is the only definite reference which indicates its importance as a silk-weaving centre. Hiuen Tsang, the Chinese pilgrim who visited Varanasi and stayed at Sarnath in the seventh century A.D., makes no mention of its silk industry though he describes the weavers of Mathura who produced a fine striped variety of cotton.

Someshwara, the Chalukya king (A.D. 1124–1138), in his work on Indian art and craft, *Manasollasa*,[29] gives a long list of fabrics woven for the king, and their place of origin. The definitely Indian names in this list are: *Nagapattana* (Negapatam) in the Chola country, *Ahilavada* (Ahalillapataka) in Gujarat, *Mulasthana* (Multan) in Punjab, *Kalinga* (Orissa) and *Vanga* (Bengal).

Ibn Said, the thirteenth century Muslim chronicler, testifies that Malabar was famous for the washing and dyeing of fabrics, and that it exported *lainas* (coloured silk or cotton material). Chau Ju Kua, a Chinese official A.D. 1225, includes 'cotton stuff with coloured silk threads' and other such textiles among the products of the Chola dominion.[30] He may have been referring to the striped *mashru* fabrics also made in Gujarat. The Venetian traveller, Marco Polo and the Arab chronicler Al Newayri, both of whom visited India in the thirteenth century, wrote about the fine textiles of Gujarat called *baroji* and *kambayati*, made at or traded from Baroch and Cambay.[31]

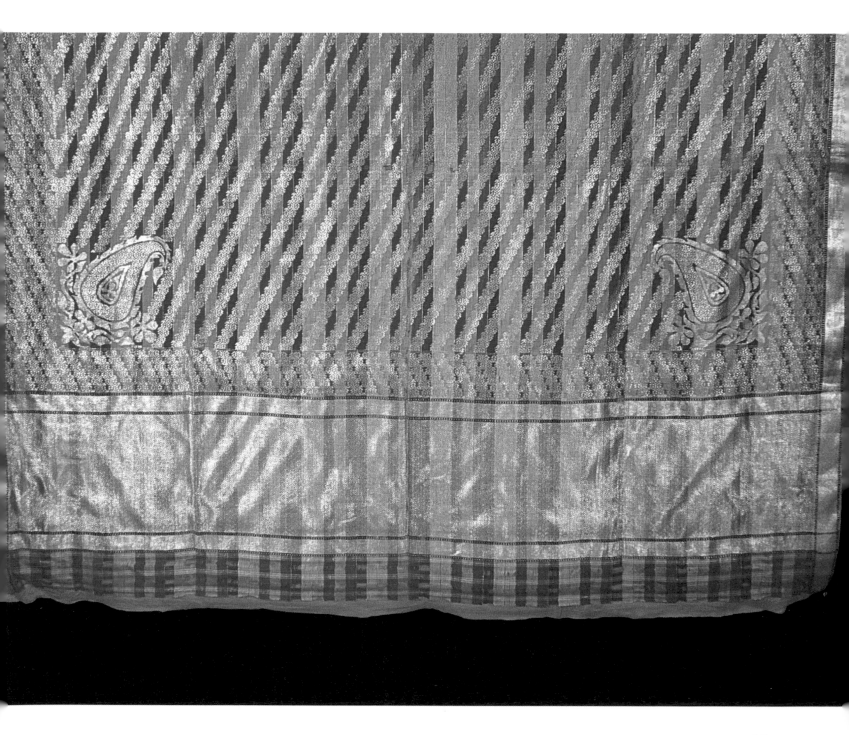

The fabrics shown in Jain, Gujarati or western Indian paintings gives us some idea of the *zari* or brocade textiles of the fifteenth century. The *dupattas* (long scarves), skirts and blouses of the ladies are decorated with golden motifs of swans, checks, stripes, flowers or dots. These diaphanous *dupattas* remind one of the silk-gauze fabrics made in Chanderi (Plate 5) and Varanasi (Plate 32). Durate Barbosa, a Portuguese who visited Gujarat between A.D. 1500–1516, was impressed by the rich silk saris worn by the women.[32]

Abul Fazl, in his biography of Akbar, the *Ain-i-Akbari,* gives a complete list of fabrics popular in that period, including silk brocades made in India, Persia, Central Asia and Turkey. In his son and successor Jahangir's autobiography, the *Tujuk-i-Jahangiri,* there is a reference to a short-sleeved jacket called *nadiri,* a fine garment made of brocade, which was introduced by Jahangir. The miniature paintings in the *Padshahnama,* the biography of Shahjahan, exhibit varieties of textiles popular during that period – the beautifully dressed royal figures and courtiers are shown wearing brocade *patkas, jamas* or *nadiris.* The accounts of some European travellers like the Italian Niccolo Manucci, and the French François Bernier and Jean-Baptiste Tavernier who visited India in the seventeenth century during the reign of Aurangzeb refer to the Indian textile industry of that period. Tavernier mentions the silk trade in Bengal, and calls Surat the centre for the weaving of silk and *zari* brocade furnishing material.

References

1. *Atharvaveda*, XVIII, 4,31.
2. *Shaunak Samhita* (*Atharvaveda*) 5,7,10. p. 102.
3. *Aranyaka, Jaimeniya Samhita* (*Samveda*).
4. *Rigveda Samhita*, 8,31,8, *Aitereya Brahmana*.
5. Maybe the English word 'drape' originated from this. It has more or less the same meaning.
6. *Sanskrit English Dictionary*, M. Monier-Williams.
7. *Shatapatha Brahmana*, 5,2,1,8 and *Katyayana Shrautasutra* 14,5,2, *St. Petersburg Dictionary* by Otto Bohtlingh and Rudolph Roth.
8. *Sanskrit English Dictionary*, M. Monier-Williams.
9. *Perspectives in the Social and Economic History of Early India*, R.S. Sharma, p. 176.
10. May have orginated from the word *shat,* the dictionary (M. Monier-Williams) meaning of which is a strip of cloth, a kind of petticoat, or a particular type of garment.
11. Made from the cocoons of non-mulberry-eating silkworms – *tassar, munga* and *eri* are varieties of silk of this category.
12. Even today the silkworm-rearing tribe of Bengal is called Punda.
13. *A Monograph on Silk Fabrics,* Yusuf Ali, p. 4. The wild silk grown around the Raipur and Bilaspur area of Chhattisgarh is known as *kosa* even today.
14. *Sutrapat,* 4,3,42.
15. *Pradeep,* Katyayana, Part 4, p. 342.
16. Megasthenes, the Greek writer and ambassador to the court of Chandragupta Maurya, refers to gorgeous embroidered robes. *History of India,* K.A.N. Sastri, Part I, p. 264.
17. Strabo, XV, 6.69: *Ashoka and the Mauryan Empire*, R. Thapar, p. 74.
18. Kautilya's *Arthashashtra,* translated by R. Shamasastry, p. 125.
19. *Arthashashtra,* 2:11: 106-109.
20. Except in Shantideva's *Sikshasamuchchaya,* seventh century A.D.
21. *Sanskrit English Dictionary,* M. Monier-Williams.
22. This may be similar to the *tashi* fabrics of a later period.
23. The word Kashgar may be derived from the weavers (*kash+gars*) of shining material.
24. Later known as *tanta* in Bengal.
25. *Prachin Bhartiya Vesh Bhusa*, Dr Motichandra, p. 156.
26. Ibid.
27. *Kadambari,* Banbhatta, translated by V.S. Agrawal, p. 182.
28. Ibid, pp. 76-85.
29. *Manasollasa,* ed. by G.K. Shrigondekar, Vol. II, Baroda, 1739, pp. 17-20, 55, 88, quoted by Dr Motichandra in 'Indian Costume and Textile from the Eighth to the Twelfth Centuries', in the *Journal of Indian Textile History*, Vol. 5, p. 21.
30. *Struggle for Empire,* ed. R.C. Mazumdar, p. 519.
31. Ibid. p. 518.
32. *Banaras Brocades,* Rai A. Krishna and V. Krishna, p. 24

Facing page

■ Plate: 5
PATKA, CHANDERI, MID-19TH CENTURY. THE SANDALWOOD OR SANDALI COLOUR SILK GAUZE WITH THE ZARI BORDER ON EITHER SIDE IS TUCKED SO DEFTLY THAT IT LOOKS LIKE IT WAS WOVEN WITH THE PIECE.

ANCIENT AND MEDIEVAL SILK FABRICS

Kausheya seems to have been the most popular of Indian silk fabrics. It was also used by the Buddhist monks of China and Central Asia, in spite of these being silk-producing regions. In the *Amarkosh,* the eighth-century Sanskrit dictionary, this is described as fabric made from the yarn obtained from the cocoons of silkworms. The quality of the yarn was rough because the silk was obtained from the cocoon after the silkworm had vacated it, piercing through it. Thus the inside silk threads are cut and had to be spun to make a long thread.

Pattron was wild silk, largely produced in Assam, Bengal and Bihar, and was categorised as a precious textile. Yarn (of varied colours) made from the cocoons of silkworms reared on different trees gave their colours to *pattron*. Kautilya mentions in the *Arthashashtra* (2.71) that *pattron* made from the cocoons of silkworms reared on the *nagkesar* was yellow; from *likucha,* wheatish; and from *molsari* and *vat* (banyan), white.

Other fine fabrics in ancient India were *dukula* and *netra*. Dr Motichandra identifies *netra* as the thick and strong silk which was made in Bengal till the fourteenth century. Mention is also made of its use as furnishing material for canopies, curtains, mattresses and spreads. For example, in the *Tilak Manjari* of Dhanpal, (a Sanskrit text of the early eleventh century), a canopy of shining *netra*[1] is mentioned, and Jyotishwar Thakur (a Maithili poet of the fourteenth century), in his work, the *Varna Ratnakar,* refers to *netra* as a bedspread or the covering of a mattress. In the Gujarati *Varnaka Samuchchaya,* *netra* is categorised as furnishing material. Medieval poets such as Malik Mohammad Jayasi and Vidyapati have also praised the richness of curtains and floorspreads made of *netra*. Ahmedabad and Surat were famed for heavy gold brocade furnishing fabrics till the late eighteenth century (Plate 6)[1]. They were very popular in the Mughal court, as seen in Mughal paintings. *Netra* was usually white, but it was also made in black, blue, violet and golden. (Banbhatta referred to *netra* as white silk with a flowered pattern.) It was also used as a decorative border on ladies' *kanchukis* (bodices). *Pinga* or *priga* was another variety of floral patterned silk – mentioned in the Kharoshti script of Central Asia. Later it was known as damask silk.[2]

Shining, decorative borders were the main design on Indian garments such as saris, *patkas*, dhotis and turbans. The borders and the *pallus* (end pieces) of these were usually woven with silk and gold or silver thread, while the remaining fabric was of fine cotton – this was a special feature of Indian brocades, and suited the dressing style of the time, as well as Indian climatic conditions. New attire, such as tunics, trousers, coats, overcoats, embroidered coats, conical hats and long-sleeved tunics, introduced by the Indo-Scythians in the early Christian era, were also responsible for the development of brocade of a thicker quality required for these kinds of clothes.

The Persians excelled in making material heavily decorated with gold and silver thread, meant only for royalty – well-known examples were *deba* or *debag* and *stavaraka*. *Stavaraka,* an ancient Pahlavi word used by the Sassanians for fine gold or silver brocades, can be categorised as *kinkhwab*. *Stavaraka* in later Persian was pronounced as *stabrak*, while in Arabic it was called *istavraka*. According to a commentator of the Quran, the word was of foreign origin (old Pahlavi) and referred to fabrics fit for dressing celestial maidens.[3] The *udichya vesha,* which was the dress of the people of the northern lands and was brought to India by them, was made of heavy material like gold and silver silk brocades. *Stavaraka* fabric was in great demand in every royal court of the time, including that of the Gupta kings of India.

Sir Aurel Stein, during his excavation of the Turfan site in the northern part of the silk route, found many examples of figured silk brocade with designs peculiar to the silks produced in Iran and elsewhere in the Near East during the period between the third and seventh centuries A.D. These Sassanian figured silks found in Turfan were used as face covers for the dead – one such pattern is a finely designed boar's head within the typical Sassanian pearl border. Pearl-bordered figured silk can be categorised with the *tarmukta stavaraka* mentioned by Banbhatta, which was used as a decorative fabric during the marriage of Princess Rajyashri (in the seventh century A.D.).

Literary references to fabrics such as *chinanshuka*, *chinachaloka* or *chinapatta* confirm their Chinese origin and trade relations between the two major textile producing countries in ancient times. The spread of Buddhism also brought these countries closer, socially and culturally. There are innumerable references to Chinese monks and piligrims visiting the land of Buddha. They usually came by the silk route taken by the traders.

M. Lombard, in his book, *Les Textiles Dans Le Monde Musulman*, has referred to the fine textiles and brocades popular in medieval times, particularly in Muslim courts. Some of these have also been mentioned by Abul Fazal in the *Ain-i-Akbari*. According to him, *sigillatos,* also known as *siqlat* or *saqallat,* was the scarlet broadcloth made in the weaving centres of ancient Greece, Byzantium, and Mesopotamia. In Mesopotamia, it was decorated with a *hawtim* (seal) or a roundel. From the sixth century A.D., *siglat* or *siqlat* was made of silk in Antioch (north Syria) with a similar pattern. Later on, the Muslims also favoured textiles decorated with roundel motifs and called them *muhattam*. Seventh-century *hadis* (or Hadith) refer to a silken head gear called *sigillat*. In the Sassanid and Byzantium centres, textiles decorated with circular

Preceding page

■ Plate: 6
PARAPET COVER, GUJARAT, 18TH CENTURY. THE OBLONG PIECE HAS A *ZARI* GROUND WITH A *MINAKARI* FLORAL *ZAL*. THE PATTERN FORMAT IS ADAPTED FROM THE PERSIAN CARPET STYLE, WHICH WAS ALSO NOTICED IN THE *PURMATAN CHAUKARAS* AND *DUPATTAS* OF VARANASI.

patterns were called *pallia rotaia* or 'rounded straw'. This design matches the patterned textiles shown in the Ajanta cave paintings. In the ninth and tenth centuries, a silk brocade from Byzantium, with a design of little circles (like copper and gold coins), was called *mudannas* – a continuity of this pattern is seen in the *asharfi buti* (gold-coin) patterned brocades of Gujarat and Varanasi.

Sakalat or *saklat* is mentioned by Jyotishwar Thakur in the *Varna Ratnakar* as a fabric of foreign origin,[4] used mostly as furnishing material and for the garments of musicians, courtiers, and so forth.

Dibag or *deba* was another exclusive textile, a silk brocade decorated with gold and silver, probably made in Sassanid Persia. It is described as a fine silk fabric, with a warp and weft of strong threads (*pakka*).[5]

The epithet *husrawani* attached to itlater, suggests the place of its origin as Khurasan in Persia. Yezd, the well-known centre for such fabrics, was a city in Khurasan province. It seems *husrawani* was a coveted fabric in India and China, although pronounced differently. A Chinese document refers to a silk fabric, found in a tomb dated A.D. 574 in Turfan, Central Asia,[6] as *deva* brocade (*fi-po-chin*) This may have been the *deba* brocade, similar to the *devanga* or *devadushya* fabrics mentioned in ancient Indian literature. Dr Motichandra observes that 'the rare mention of *devanga* and *devadushya* in medieval literature should support the view that perhaps it was a costly material of foreign origin. It may be suggested that the first element *deva* in both *devanga* and *devadushya* may have been

■ Plate: 7
LADIES' GARMENT, GUJARAT, 19TH CENTURY. A *KINKHAB* BROCADE WITH MARIGOLD FLOWER *BUTIS*.

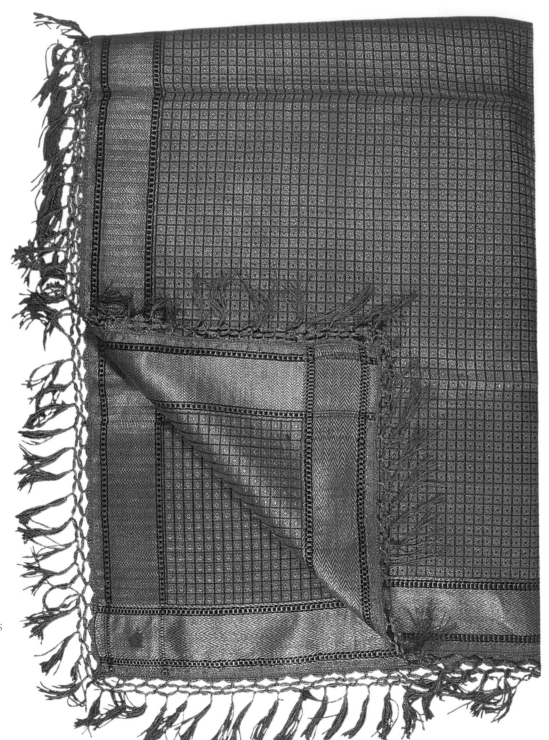

■ Plate: 8
SQUARE KERCHIEF, DOUBLE-SIDED (*DORUKHA*), VARANASI, EARLY 20TH CENTURY. THE ENTIRE GROUND IS FILLED WITH SMALL SQUARES HAVING GOLD AND SILVER DOTS INSIDE. THE PATTERN IS CALLED *BULBUL CHASHMA* OR NIGHTINGALE'S EYE. A *ZARI* BORDER WITH *MOTHRA* PATTERN IN BLACK SILK IS AROUND THE KERCHIEF.

derived from the Persian *diba* or *dibah*, the Pahlavi *depak*, the Armenian *dipak*, the Syrian *dybg*, adopted by the Arabs as *dihadj* in the time of Mohammad'.[7] But this fabric may have been of Indian origin, as the name suggests. According to the Persian dictionary, *diba* or *dibah* originated from the Arabic word *dibaq*. The root of the word is *dys*, which means brilliant or shiny in Arabic. This may have originated from the Sanskrit *divya*, which also means brilliant or most beautiful. These gold and silver-worked fabrics were probably made in the ancient Indian textile centres at Paithan, Kanchipuram, Latdesh or Mandasor, and were called *devanga* or *devadushya*. It is possible that apart from Sassanid Persia, these fabrics were also woven in the region around the Persian Gulf, Iraq and Syria, and were traded by Arabs, who referred to them by their Indian name, *devanga*, pronounced differently in Arabic.

In medieval Indian literature such as the *Samaraichchakaha* of Haribhadra, and the *Paiasddamahannavo*, *devanga* and *devadushya* are referred to as material worn by the gods and kings. Jyotishwar Thakur, in the *Varna Ratnakar*, mentions that kings wore *devanga* garments for their coronation ceremony.[8] It was also used to make curtains and canopies (*devagapata vitanaka*), as mentioned by Dhanpal in the *Tilak Manjari* (early eleventh century). *Devanga* was worn during the wedding ceremony by both the bride and the groom, the latter wore a white patterned *devanga*. Apparently, a variety of *devanga* or *deba* fabrics, both plain and patterned, and of varied textures and colours, were made in different centres and were named

accordingly. For example, *eksun* or *aksun*, a black-coloured *deba*, was a popular fabric during the Sultanate period (late thirteenth to sixteenth centuries). It was probably imported from the Caspian seaport, Abaskun, an important silk-trading centre at that time.[9] *Dibag* was of two types; the multicoloured *munaqqas* and the unicoloured *sadiq*, similar to damask satin. *Deba* fabrics were named after different centres where they were made. Ibn Batuta (A.D. 1355) mentions *dibahae chin*, a fine Chinese brocade. *Diba-e-firangi*, referred to by Abul Fazl, was brocade made at various European centres such as Spain and Italy. *Dibag* made in Spain was known as *debaza* and that made in Yezd in Persia as *diba-e-Yezdi*. Other varieties made at Susa and Tustar, or Shustar, were called *Susy* and *Tustari* respectively.

Shustari was mentioned in the cloth control regulations of Ala-ud-din Khilji, the Sultan of Delhi (A.D. 1296-1316). *Susy*, a fabric originally made at the ancient Persian town of Susiana in Shustar – was fine silk or mixed silk gauze with small checks. In India, it was made at Agra, Azamgarh and Shahjahanpur, and also in Varanasi until the early twentieth century. The fabric was probably introduced to India by *khazzaz* or *nassaj* (weavers) who had migrated there. Brocades made at Byzantine centres were called *rumi*.

Abul Fazl, in his list of textiles popular during Akbar's reign, mentions *deba* and *mushajjar* (a kind of silk brocade woven with leaves and branch patterns), made in Yezd and Europe respectively. This may have been the *diba-e-Yezdi* and *diba-e-*

■ Plate: 9
SILK FRAGMENT, CHINA,
13TH-14TH CENTURY. ZHAO
FENG IN HIS BOOK *TREASURES
IN SILK* SEES THIS AS AN
EXAMPLE OF *NASIJ*.

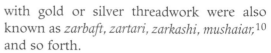

firangi, or the *munaqqas* fabric mentiond earlier.

Another ancient silk brocade called *kimha* had a pattern woven on a gold or silver background and was probably made in Mongolia or North China, from where the word *kimha* may have originated. Later, the technique and design spread to a large area, from China to Persia, where it was called *kimsa.* It also reached countries such as Byzantium, Italy, Spain and India, where it was called by different names. In Byzantium, it was called *kamokhas*; in Italy, *camoca*; in Spain, *camocan*; in France, *camocat*; and in India, *kinkhab* (Plate 7). In Persian the word *kamkhwab* means the material which comes rarely in dreams. *Tashi kinkhab* had a background of gold thread and a pattern of silver thread. Later, such work was called *ganga jamuni.* In the Sultanate period, textiles

with gold or silver threadwork were also known as *zarbaft, zartari, zarkashi, mushaiar,*[10] and so forth.

Ibn Batuta, in *Rehla,* describes how on his visit to Smyrna (Izmir, the Turkish capital) he was presented two garments made of a fabric called *kamkha,* a kind of silk made in Baghdad, Tabriz, Nishapur and China. Another writer of the Sultanate period, Ziyauddin Barani,[11] refers to *kamkha* as a costly fabric which was included in the cloth control order of Sultan Ala-ud-din. There was a category of exclusive textiles which was not meant for the common people and could not be sold in the market (*sarai adl*) without an order from the superintendent. Among the presents received by Mohammad Tughlaq from the Emperor of China were five hundred pieces of *kamkha,* of which 'a hundred were made in the town of Zaitun and the others were made in Khansa'.

In India, Gujarat was famous for brocades patterned with different coloured silk threads on a gold or silver background. The end panels of *patkas* (plate 66, page 87), *ashavali,* saris (plate 58, page 78) or *dupattas,* as well as furnishing materials (plate 6), were made using a similar technique. *Kamkhwab* was also imported from Persia and Kabul. During the Mughal period, some popular Gujarati brocades, such as *daraibaf* and *muqayyash* (silk with silver stripes), as well as *kurtahwar* (patterned or striped with gold), and *shela chira* for turbans and *dupattas* were also exported to other countries.

Zytunia, one of the finest varieties of Chinese satin silk brocades, was exported to different countries, including India, from the port of Zaytun (or Zaitun) in China. The

intricate patterns were woven with silk on a satin background. Coats or jackets made of *zytunia* were favoured by kings. Later, the fabric was copied at Persian and Syrian textile centres. The Chinese weavers, taken as prisoners after the Muslim victory at Talas (eighth century A.D.), were forced to part with their knowledge of silk weaving techniques to Persian and Syrian weavers. Damascus became particularly famous for making such highly coveted patterned satin fabrics known as 'damask satin'. Later Timur, the central Asian conqueror, deported the weavers of damask cloth from Damascus to Samarkand and Bukhara. From here, these weavers must have gone to Indian centres as well, particularly Lahore in Punjab, and Gujarat.

The famous medieval poet, Amir Khusrau, mentions a fine silk fabric called *juz* – a word of Arabic origin also pronounced as *djuzz*.[12] According to Ibn Batuta, among the presents sent to the Emperor of China by Muhammad Tughlaq, were a hundred pieces of *djuzz* silk, and one special piece woven in five colours.[13] This can be compared with the *Indrayudhazalamber* fabric mentioned by Banbhatta in the seventh century.[14] Similarly, *sahrang* was a type of material in which three colours were used. This was also used as a turban cloth. The number of colours used in weaving a textile increased its cost, as is the case even today, because the process is time-consuming and complicated.

■ Plates: 10 & 10a
CHAUKARA, DETAIL OF CORNER AND CENTRE, VARANASI, LATE 19TH CENTURY. THE SILK GAUZE GROUND IS FILLED WITH CLOSELY ARRANGED *CARRIE BUTIS*. THE ARRANGEMENT IS CALLED *ALE GALE* LOCALLY. THE SIMILARITY WITH *NASIJ* CANNOT BE IGNORED.

■ Plate: 11
SILK FRAGMENT, CHINA,
LIAO DYNASTY. A BLUE SILK
GROUND PATTERNED WITH
GOLDEN STRIPS ON ANIMAL
SUBSTRATE (LEATHER). SUCH
WOVEN OR STAMPED DESIGN
APPEARS IN EARLY CHINESE
EXAMPLES WITH DECORATIVE
ANIMAL MOTIFS. LATER, DUE
TO THE ISLAMIC INFLUENCE
THE FLORAL OR
GEOMETRICAL PATTERN
REPLACED THE ANIMALS.
(See also plate: 12)

Khuzz or *khazz* was mostly made in Khuzistan, i.e., Baghdad, Kufa, Basra, Fars, and other places in the region. During the Sultanate period, it was made in Delhi and Kotla. There are references to four thousand silk weavers called *khazzaz*, who were employed by the Delhi Sultans in their royal workshops. Apparently, the term *khazz* was used for the heavy silk brocade as well as the plush velvet material made of silk and wool.[15] The Arabic word *khazzahai* means ancient textile. It also means full of intrigue or illusion[16] perhaps because these fabrics being woven with yarns of more than one colour, gave the illusion of being multi-hued in different lights, or were woven in such a way that the obverse and reverse were of two different colours and could be used on either side (*dorukha*; Plate 8, page 24). Later, such *dorukha* or double-sided woollen shawls were made in Kashmir.

Nasij (Plate 9, page 26) was a fine silk, and the weavers who made it were called *nassaj*.[17] Amir Khusrau referred to *nasij* in his collection of poetry, *Nuh Sipihr*. Marco Polo (A.D. 1256–1323) also described the fabric. 'In Baudas (Baghdad) they weave many kinds of silk stuff and gold brocades such as *nasich (nasiz)*, *nac (nakhkh)* and *cramoisy (kirmiji)*, and many other tissues richly wrought with figures of birds and beast.'[18] Ibn Batuta observed, 'At Nishapur are made silken garments (*harir*) of *nakhkh* and velvet which are taken to India'.[19] In Persia it was also called *nachidut,* which meant a silk fabric interwoven with gold.

The words *nakkut* and *nachidut* were of Mongol origin and the plural form of *nakh* and *nachetti*. These figured fabrics may have been introduced in Baghdad and Persia during the reign of the Mongol king Halagu. According to Dr Motichandra, the fabric seems to disappear in the sixteenth century, as these terms rarely occur in the literature of the time. It may be that this material, with birds and beast motifs (Plate 11), and much liked by the Mongols (later known as the *shikargah* pattern) slowly disappeared after the establishment of a non-Mongol dynasty by Shaikh Hasan (after the death of the last Mongol king, Abu Said, in A.D. 1335). There may have been a limited clientele for this kind of figured fabric due to increasing Muslim influence, which prohibited the depiction of any living creature. The other possibility is that these fabrics were made later by weavers who migrated to other countries, and there they were known by other names. (The famous *nakshband* weavers of Varanasi probably belong to this category of weavers who were – and still are – known for making such complicated and intricate designs.)

Perniyan was a Persian brocade worn by kings, particularly on festive occasions. It was the favourite fabric of the Sassanian kings, Rustam and Zal (AD 579–642),[20] and probably had a pattern similar to that of leopard skin.[21] *Perniyan* is mentioned by Firdausi in the *Shahnama* and by Amir Khusrau in the *Qiran-us-Saidain*. 'Jama-yi-harir va parniyan' mentioned in Persian literature means upper male garment made of very fine *katan* silk fabric.

Ilaycha was striped silk fabric (Plate13, page 30), usually in red or bluish red with white stripes. The name is probably derived from the Turkish *alcha* or *alacha*. During the

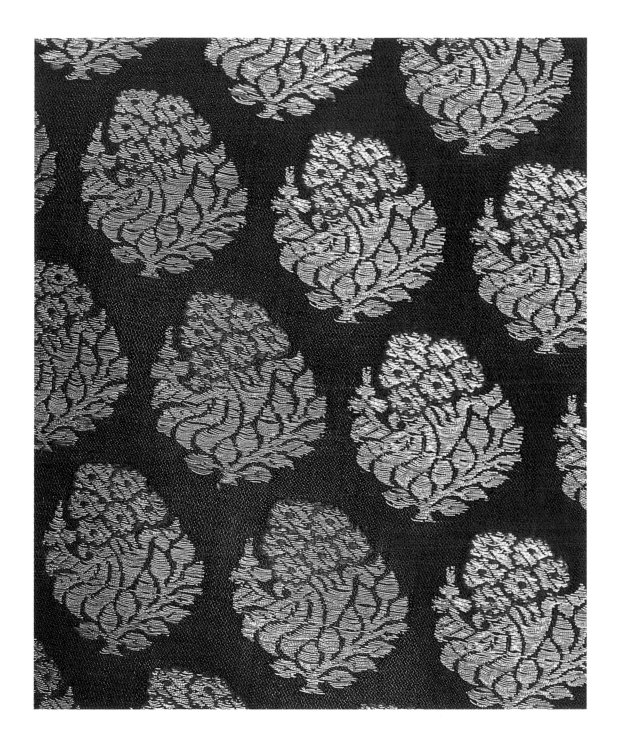

■ Plate: 12
JACKET, GUJARAT, LATE 19TH CENTURY. A DROP-SHAPED GOLD *ZARI BUTI* ON NAVY BLUE SILK GROUND; THE PATTERN CAN BE COMPARED WITH THE CHINESE EXAMPLE (PLATE 11).

ILAYCHA, SURAT, 19TH
CENTURY. SATIN MASHRU
HAVING A PATTERN WITH
THE DAGGER OR FLYING BIRD
MOTIF. FIGURES IN AJANTA
PAINTINGS ARE SHOWN
WEARING CLOTHES WITH
SIMILAR MOTIFS.

Mughal period, Agra was known for its *ilaycha* fabrics, which were mostly used to make lower-body garments, lining for brocade dresses or as furnishing. Later it was also made at other centres as the *Mashru* fabric.

Ghaltidan, a Persian word, later known as *galta,* was a mixed fabric of cotton and silk in satin weave with a design of checks, or checks and stripes, having two or three lines of different coloured silk thread. The fabric had a glazed surface because it was passed through hot rolling cylinders. Its well-pressed and calendered upper surface showed the silk, and the back, the cotton. This west Asian fabric was introduced in India and became a speciality of Azamgarh, Mau, Mubarakpur and Kairabad. Later, it was also woven in Varanasi (in Badibazar) by weavers who had migrated there from Mau.

Daryayi silk is mentioned in Abul Fazl's list. It was a twelve-inch-wide, green, red, yellow, blue and white fabric used mainly by Hindus as a *patka* in their wedding ceremonies, or as a border for women's garments. *Daryayi* was made in Meerut and Lucknow till the late nineteenth century by weavers called *daryayi baff*, who had probably migrated to India from the region between Syr Darya and Amu Darya in Central Asia, which was a well-known silk-weaving area. It may have also derived its name from the striped or wavy pattern of the fabric.

Indian brocades are also usually referred to by the place where they are made, as in the case of *Ashavali* saris which were made in ancient Ashaval, (modern Ahmedabad), *ahinavala* silk (made in Anahilawada, in Patan, north Gujarat), and *chakresvari* silk (made in the village Chakrabari in Howrah district, Bengal), mentioned by Jyotishwar Thakur in the *Varna Ratnakar*. *Dandaprakara*, another kind of silk mentioned, was apparently a striped fabric. He also gives a list of silk fabrics such as *deva, sevanga, senasuri, gadipali, gajipalli, sonapal,* and so forth, which were used to make garments like the *kaba* or *qaba* (a long, loose coat).

Tashi, atlas and *kakum* were other popular varieties of silk brocades. *Tashi* was a fabric made with flat gold and silver thread (this was also made in ancient times). *Atlas* was a satin brocade with a monochrome pattern and had no *zari* in it. Made in most of the known weaving centres, its colours were usually deep red, green, white, and later black. *Kakum* was a decorative border, popular during the reign of Mohammad Tuglaq, who preferred wearing robes of plain material decorated with borders only. Such borders were made both in Persia and India and were also called *sanjab*. They were an essential part of any stitched garment and enhanced its beauty.

References

1. This may have been similar to *hiranyakashipu*, mentioned in Vedic literature. Later, Gujarat was known for making such fabrics.
2. Agrawal, V.S., *Harsh Charit Ek Sanskrit Adhyayan*, p. 79.
3. Akhtar, Dr Shamim, Professor, Persian Department, Banaras Hindu University.
4. Thakur, Jyotishwar, *Varna Ratnakar*, p. 22, eds. Chatterjee S.K. and Babua Misra, 1943.
5. Mohammad, Maulavi Qubul *Hafat-e-Qulzum* (Persian Dictionary), Vol. II, p. 171.
6. Liu, Xinru, *Silk and Religion*, p. 51. The author has identified it as Indian brocade.
7. Dr Motichandra, Indian Costume and Textile from the Eighth to the Twelfth Centuries, *Journal of Indian Textile History* No. V, p. 14, 1960.
8. Thakur Jyotishwar, *Varna Ratnakar*, p. 22, eds. Chatterjee S.K. and Babua Misra, 1942.
9. Mohammad, Maulavi Qubul *Hafat-e-Qulzum* (Persian dictionary), Vol. II, p. 171.
10. Motichandra, Costume and Textile in the Sultanate Period, *Journal of Indian Textile History*, Vol. VI, p. 18, 1961.
11. *Tarikh Firuzshahi*, pp. 309 - 312.
12. This Arabic word probably originated from the Persian word *jauz*. In the *Gayasul Logat, jauz* is referred to 'as the brightest star among all the other stars in the sky'. It may be that star-patterned brocades were called *jauz*. Perhaps *juz* was a fine Persian brocade made at other centres too. Another meaning of *jauz*, given in the dictionary, is a black sheep with white stripes – *juz* is striped, though not necessarily only with white stripes. It can be the striped *Mashru*.
13. *Ars Islamica*, XI-XII, p. 137, Art Journal of Michigan University, published 1934-1951.
14. It may be a fabric with a rainbow-coloured pattern.
15. Batuta, Ibn, *Rehla*, Tr 2, p. 151.
16. Information given by Dr Naseema Faruki, Reader, Arabic Department, Banaras Hindu University.
17. *Logat-e-Kishai*, Persian Dictionary.
18. Polo, Marco, p. 65.
19. *Ars Islamica*, XI-XII, p. 116.
20. Mohammad, Maulavi Qubul, *Hafat-e-Qulzum*, Persian Dictionary, Vol. I.
21. Ibid.

EXPANSION OF THE SILK BROCADE INDUSTRY

The spread of Chinese mulberry silk (and the art of weaving it) to cities of other ancient civilisations revolutionised the world's weaving industry.[1] The Chinese silk industry was highly organised and supported by the state which made silk into a veritable cash crop. China was exporting silk as early as the second century B.C. and remained the major silk producer for centuries. The Chinese emperor, Wu-Ti (140–87 B.C.), realised the importance of expanding the silk trade to distant countries.[2] Thus, a trade route was opened from China to West Asia, through Tarim Basin to the territories in the Oxus region, forcing back the Huns (who intercepted the traders on the silk route) to the north. The route was secured by the Chinese army, often accompanied by a Chinese political mission and traders, who visited distant places like Bactria and Persia. The fine silk fabrics and silk yarn also reached the Mediterranean through Parthia and Syria, and carried the fame of the 'silk-weaving Seres' (Chinese) to the great centres of the Greek and Roman civilisations. Thus silk became the industrial wealth of China, and its production was a jealously guarded secret so that it could retain its monopoly of the trade. The weaving of the fine silk fabrics required intensive labour, specialised technology and division of labour that individual peasant households, or even professional weavers, could not afford. Such textiles were made under royal patronage in royal workshops. In China, silk fabrics were reserved for the exclusive use of the royal family, the nobility and officials – a practice followed in other countries too, including India during the Sultanate and Mughal periods.

The Sassanids, realising its trade potential, became intermediaries for the Chinese silk trade. Silk, both woven and raw, was traded to Mediterranean countries via Parthia and Syria, from where it made its way to Europe. Silk fabrics, influenced by Chinese prototypes, were also woven in the Sassanian weaving centres of Khurasan, Kashan and other places. Soon these silk brocades became known for their beauty and were exported to other countries. Sassanids were mainly responsible for the export of silk from the East to the West. Even their dynasty's founder, Ardeshir, was the son of a silk merchant.

Sericulture was taken outside China in the second century A.D. According to legend, it was smuggled out by a Chinese princess who was married to a prince of Khotan in Central Asia. She hid the silk cocoons in her coiffure and took them to

■ Plate: 15
SILK FRAGMENT, PERSIA,
17TH CENTURY, BROCADE.
ONE OF THE FINEST
EXAMPLES OF PERSIAN
BROCADE AND THE WORK OF
A MASTER CRAFTSMAN. USE
OF MORE THAN ONE-COLOUR
SILK IN DESIGN GIVES IT A
PAINTING-LIKE FINISH. THE
GROUND IS DECORATED WITH
LOZENGE-SHAPED IMPRESS
WORK KNOWN AS *UTTU*, A
TECHNIQUE SEEN IN PERSIAN
BROCADES AND LATER ON
INDIAN BROCADES TOO.

Preceding page 32

■ Plate: 14
CHOGA, LATE 18TH OR EARLY
19TH CENTURY. THE *CARRIE*
PATTERN IS MADE WITH
SILVER *ZARI* AND COLOURED
SILK *MINAKARI* ON A *KATAN*
SILK GROUND. THERE IS A
TUCKED *SANJAB* (*SINJAB*)
BORDER AT THE EDGES.
CARRIE BECAME A POPULAR
MOTIF FROM THE 18TH
CENTURY.

her adopted country.[3] The introduction of sericulture made Khotan prosperous. The Princess was deified by the people and a temple was built in her honour, which was described by the Chinese traveller Hiuen Tsang in the seventh century.

Silk weaving became popular in other areas as well, particularly in Persia, and in the region around Syr Darya and Oxus rivers. Khotan, Bulkh, Kashgar, Bukhara, Khurasan, Kashan, Damascus, and Gujarat in India became the known centres. The similarity between Gujarati, Sassanian and ancient Greek motifs provides interesting material for study, especially when seen in a historical perspective. This may have been the result of interaction with Greek traders in ancient times, or may have been passed on by the Sassanians, who were actually Achaemenians,[4] settled around the Persian Gulf in the pre-Christian era. They were known for their refined sartorial taste. The Sassanid[5] rulers of Persia reached a high degree of achievement in various art forms, especially that of weaving. They used a shuttle for weaving patterns – the well-known pattern-weaving technique of the later period.

Eastern and southern Iran was the heart of the silk industry during this period – some of the key cities were in the province of Khurasan, such as Yezd, Kashan (north of Isfahan) and Merv. They were known for their high-quality brocades made in the Chinese style. Ibn-al-Faqih said (in A.D. 903), 'considering the good quality of its textiles one would think that Khurasan is a province of China'. This is proof of the strong Chinese influence on the designs and techniques adopted by Khurasan's textile industry – primarily because of Sassanian involvement in the silk trade, and later due to Mongolian rule in the region from A.D. 1258 to 1335.

Apparently Persian weavers were in great demand, and many of them migrated to other countries to seek employment in royal workshops, and later to escape the atrocities perpetrated by the invading Muslims. One such group of sun worshippers migrated from southern Persia (Faristan) to Saurashtra in Gujarat and are called Parsis in India. The weavers among them must have introduced to this region the Sassanian motifs and techniques popular in their own

country, as are seen in their fabrics. Since they came from the area around the Persian Gulf, known for its high-quality pearls, their beautiful embroidered borders use real pearls.[6] Gujarati fabrics greatly affected the rest of the Indian brocade industry as far as technique and design were concerned – migrating Gujarati weavers were responsible for setting up many new weaving centres and re-enforcing existing ones.

During the reign of Sultan Khudabanda (A.D. 1300-1335), the son of Halaku, in Persia, silk fabrics of the region known as Mazindaran (south of the Caspian Sea) became famous, and were available in the markets of other big cities. Many Indian weavers from Mandasor, Bharuch, and Paithan were also invited to work in Sassanian workshops in Susa, Gundeshpur and Shustar.

Satin weave was also introduced by Persian weavers,[7] first in Gujarat, and later in other weaving centres. Gujarati motifs, such as undulating floral creepers (Plate 63, page 84), curving leaves and buds, and female dolls, either standing or dancing, (referred to as *putlis;* Plates 59, 65, pages 80, 86) are reminiscent of the Achaemenian tradition.[8]

Sassanid (third to seventh centuries A.D.) textiles, which greatly influenced Indian silk brocades of a later period, were known for their beauty and unique patterns. The

Left

■ Plate: 16
SILK FRAGMENT, PERSIA, MID 17TH CENTURY, BROCADE. THE POPPY PLANT ON SILVER METALLIC GROUND.

Right

■ Plate: 17
SILK FRAGMENT, GUJARAT/ PERSIA, 17TH CENTURY. A TULIP PLANT ON A SILVER GROUND IS EMBOSSED WITH *UTTU* WORK.

Left

■ Plate: 18
SILK FRAGMENT, PERSIA,
18TH CENTURY, BROCADE.
FLOWERING PLANT GROWING
ON A MOUND AGAINST A
METALLIC GROUND.

Right

■ Plate: 19
SILK FRAGMENT, MUGHAL,
18TH CENTURY. *ZARI* AND
MINAKARI ARE BUILT ON A
SILK GROUND; FROM
STYLISED ROCKS AT THE
BOTTOM EMERGES THE
FLOWERING PLANT.

designs were the result of a fusion of three ancient textile traditions – the Mesopotamian, Chinese and Hellenic. The migration of the Sassanid weavers to China, Central Asia and India, along the silk route, brought them into close contact with the local technique and designs of these regions, from which they assimilated many characteristics. The Indian element in the designs of these textiles was mainly due, however, to the expansion of Buddhism in the area, and motifs used extensively in different forms were the lotus, lion, bull, elephant, tree of life, and vase of plenty among others.

Common Indian and west Asian motifs were popular since the Mauryan and Sunga periods (third to first centuries B.C.). During the Kushan period (first to third centuries A.D.) who ruled north India, part of Afghanisan and central Asia (Gandhar, Khotan, Balkh etc.), the continental trading and diplomatic silk route ran across the Parthian and Kushan dominions. The union of people of central Asia, Afghanistan, India (including present Pakistan) and eastern Iran within the framework of a single state and their comparative security from foreign invasion led to flourishing trade and great prosperity in this region. Indian traders profited from the exchange between the Mediterranean countries and east Asia. They

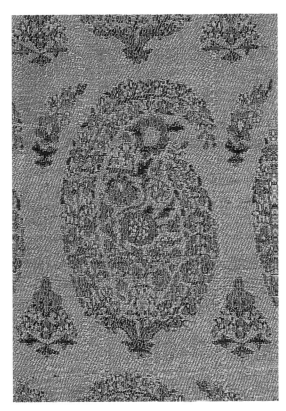

procured Chinese silk, which was sold to the Romans with Indian cotton textiles, spices, crystal, lapis lazuli and glassware[9]. The Gupta kings (fourth to sixth centuries A.D.), known for their splendid cultural achievements, also actively encouraged cultural and religious exchanges. There was a regular flow of Buddhist pilgrims from China to India, who brought with them silk as coveted gifts for the Indian rulers. (Silk weaving was already well established in India, which is testified by the temple inscription at Mandasor.)[10]

The extensive use of silk, especially Chinese silk for clothing and other purposes, made India an open market for silk imports. With all the Indian-made kausheya available, Indian rulers and the elite still craved for Chinese silks. Envoys from the kingdoms of northwest India (Balkh, Taxila, or the Sirhind region, which were linked by Central Asian routes to China), as well as south India (which was linked by sea routes), were often sent to the T'ang rulers (A.D. 618-907) in China with gifts from India. The envoys returned with Chinese silk, robes of brocade and other gifts from China.[11] Someshwar, in his *Manasollasa* (twelfth century), listed 'Mahachina' as a centre for the production of silk along with Indian silk-weaving centres.

From the fourth and fifth centuries onwards, China no longer remained the sole

Left

■ Plate: 20
SILK FRAGMENT, PERSIA, 18TH CENTURY. THE LEAF PATTERN IS BROUGHT OUT BY THE *URTU* TECHNIQUE, COMMON IN 19TH-CENTURY BANARAS BROCADES.

Right

■ Plate: 21
SILK FRAGMENT, PERSIA, 18TH-19TH CENTURY, THE *BOTEH* OR *BUTA* PALMETTES CALLED *CARRIE* IN INDIA. THIS IS ONE OF THE MOST CELEBRATED PATTERNS USED IN INDIAN TEXTILES FROM THE 18TH CENTURY.

■ Plate: 22
SASH END PANEL, PERSIA,
18TH CENTURY. NARCISSUS
PLANTS EDGED BY A FLORAL
BORDER - A SIMILAR PATTERN
IS FOUND ON SOME KASHMIRI
SHAWLS.

producer of fine silk textiles. Many countries begun to make polychrome-patterned silk (which had originated in China),[12] although the Chinese retained their monopoly on thin, translucent silk fabric. While Chinese patterned silk remained in great demand in various countries, products from the central Asian states, Sassanid Persia, Byzantium and India also reached the foreign markets – care was taken to make fabrics with patterns which were popular in the country where they were being exported. During the sixth century A.D., Sassanian polychrome silk became very famous. These were the most sought-after gifts, presented to emperors by envoys and traders. Khurasan was renowned for this fabric, which later influenced Indian silk brocades.

Two Persian empires, the Achaemenids (fourth to fifth centuries B.C.) and Sassanids (third to seventh centuries A.D.), disseminated Persian customs and ideas across the vast area between the Mediterranean Sea and the Indus River. The highly refined synthesis of culture which prevailed in the eastern Iranian region of Khurasan and Transoxiana formed the basis of Islamic culture in later centuries.

Widespread Muslim invasions from the seventh century[13] and the establishment of Muslim kingdoms by the Arabs and Turks of Central Asia, who by religious zeal and

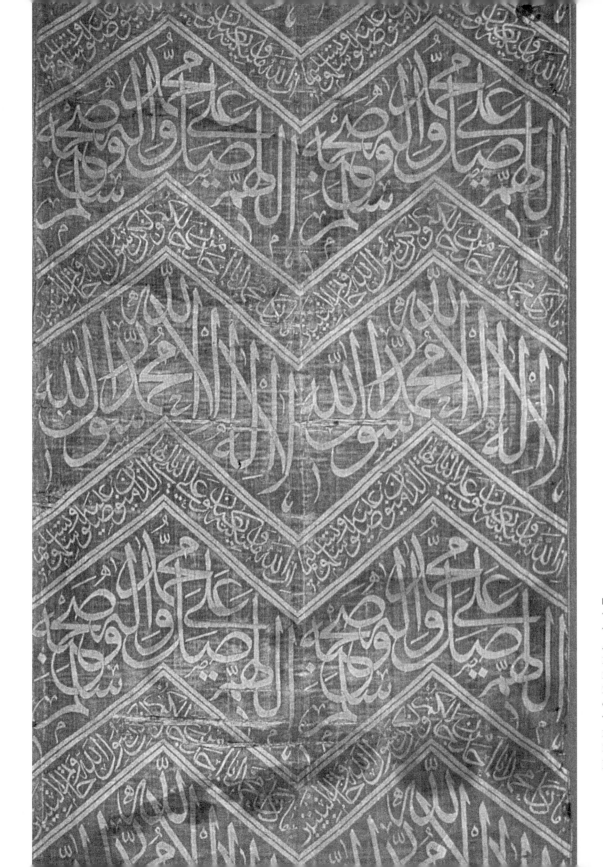

■ Plate: 23
TOMB COVER FRAGMENT, TURKEY, 17-18TH CENTURY, *LAMPAS*. QURANIC INSCRIPTIONS ARE ARRANGED IN CHEVRON, A MOTIF POPULAR IN THE 19TH CENTURY BANARAS BROCADES THAT WAS REPLACED BY A FLORAL OR GEOMETRICAL PATTERN (see plate 30, page 50).

■ Plate: 24
PURSE, LATE 19TH CENTURY, CHINA. ROOSTERS AND PARROTS WITH THE DECORATIVE FLORAL CREEPER ON RED SATIN GROUND. STYLISED ANIMALS BELONGED TO ANCIENT CHINESE PATTERNS AND INFLUENCED THE BROCADE PATTERNS OF OTHER REGIONS. THE EMBROIDERED 'PARSI BORDER' TUCKED ON THE SARI WORN BY THE PARSI LADIES IN INDIA IS INFLUENCED BY THIS PATTERN.

41

conquest carved out the most powerful and wealthiest nations of medieval times and unified a large area comprising central, west and south Asian and a few Mediterranean countries into an Islamic empire. With other material culture of the conquered lands, they inherited the silk industry also. Their influence was felt on the woven fabrics and the mode of dress. Also, in the tent culture of the Arabs and Turks, textiles played an important part as furnishing items. With rising Muslim power, cities grew and the new aristocracy residing in these demanded luxurious textiles which required more workshops and meant more opportunities for the weavers.

Though old centres continued producing silk brocades, new centres came up too because of the mass migration of weavers. Technique and designs were exhanged freely among them which was ideal for the development of the silk brocade industry. Textiles made at these centres were exported to other countries as well.

It is interesting to note how various patterns and techniques were taken to distant countries from the place of their origin, either through trade or by migrating weavers. The original motifs were often modified according to the requirements of the place.

The Ghaznavids (Turks from Ghazni), brought Islamic culture to India during the eleventh to twelfth centuries. Mahmud Ghaznavi invaded India several times from A.D. 1000 onwards. Though he looted the wealth of India, and forced many to convert to Islam, he never ruled the country. Punjab, however, was a province of the Ghazni empire, and in A.D. 1031, Mahmud's son Masud appointed Ahmed Niyaltigin as the governor of the province. He made Lahore its capital, and turned it into another centre of Islamic culture. 'Poets and scholars from Kashgar, Bukhara, Samarkand, Baghdad, Nishapur and Ghazni congregated in Lahore. Thus, the Turko-Persian Islamic culture of Khurasan and Transoxiana was brought deep into India; it would be taken further in the thirteenth century.'[14] (There were five hundred weavers of gold tissue in the service of the Sultan, who made gold brocades for the royal household and the nobility.)

After the Ghaznavids, the Ghoris from the Hindukush mountains became the new rulers of India, making Delhi their capital. Delhi became another cultural centre, enriched by artists, craftsmen, scholars, architects, musicians and others who had fled the devastation wreaked by the Mongols on Transoxiana and Khurasan. 'After the sack of Baghdad by the Mongols in A.D. 1258, Delhi became the most important cultural centre of the Muslim east.'[15] According to Ibn Batuta's description of the Delhi court during the reign of Mohammad Tughlaq, 'the state gave liberal encouragement to industry. There was a state manufactory in which four hundred silk weavers were employed, and stuff of all kinds was prepared'.[16]

The Muslim rulers of Delhi (the Ghaznavids, Ghoris, Khiljis, Lodhis and Mughals), and the Bahamani kings of the Deccan, modelled their lifestyle on that of

Facing page

■ Plate: 25
KAFTAN FRAGMENT, TURKEY, 16TH CENTURY, LAMPAS. OGIVAL TRELLIS OF TULIPS AND CARNATIONS WERE MOSTLY USED AS FURNISHING FABRICS. THEY WERE POPULAR IN THE MUGHAL COURT TOO AND TURKISH PATTERNS LIKE THEM WERE THE PROTOTYPE OF THE BADRUM JAL PATTERN OF INDIAN BROCADES.

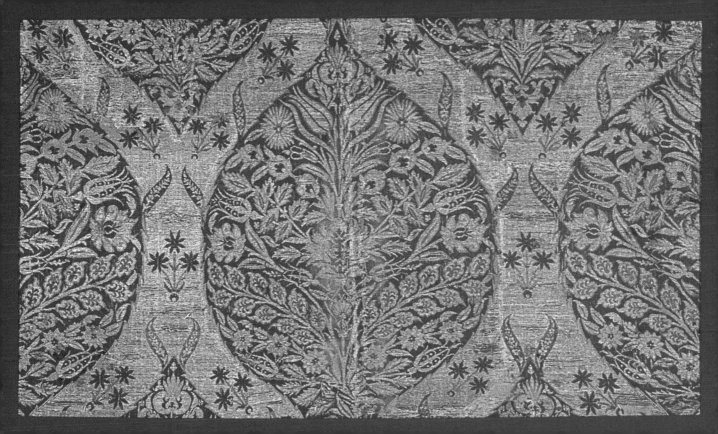

Right

■ Plate: 26
KESA, BUDDHIST MONK'S ROBE, JAPAN, EARLY 19TH CENTURY. SUCH FLOATING FLORAL PATTERNS (HERE PEONIES WITH LEAVES) WERE REFERRED TO AS *BAITHI BUTI* OR RECLINING PATTERN IN VARANASI.

Bottom

■ Plate: 27
SILK FRAGMENT, BROCADE, 19TH CENTURY, GUJARAT. THE PATTERN IS DIVIDED INTO AN UPPER AND LOWER PART, THE FLOWER LOOKS LIKE A STYLISED CHINESE CLOUD DONE IN SILVER *ZARI* OUTLINED WITH BLACK.

the Turkish and Persian upper classes, who predominated in western and central Asia. As a result, an eclectic art emerged in the Indian subcontinent, which contained the ingredients of three major civilisations, each making its own contribution. Indian, Persian and central Asian or Chinese art techniques were adopted, and blended in with local ones, and the trade or exchange of the best commodities from these countries set a high standard for artistic endeavour. Marco Polo and Ibn Batuta both speak of ports which were visited by merchants from foreign countries such as Bharuch in Gujarat and Calicut in Kerala. Ibn Batuta mentions a Saiyyad Abdul Hasan Abadi, who conducted long-term business transactions with southern states and brought goods for the king from Iraq and Khurasan.[17] Durate Barbosa, a Portuguese traveller, visited Vijaynagar in A.D. 1516, and described the city as a seat of active commerce.

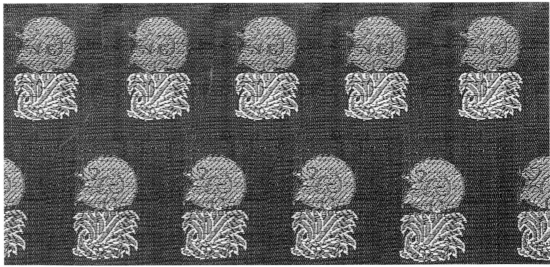

References

1. The rearing of silk cocoons was developed by Neolithic farmers living along the Hwang Ho river in northern China, more than four thousand years ago.

2. Stein, Sir Aurel, *On Ancient Central Asian Tracks*, p. 17-20.

3. A painted panel now in the British Museum excavated at the site of Dandan Oilik (district Khotan) by Sir Aurel Stein, is the visual narration of the story. In the Graeco-Buddhist style of the first and second centuries A.D. It shows a richly dressed lady with a high diadem on her head and a basketful of silk cocoons.

4. Inhabitant of Achaea, a northern district in the Greek island of Peloponnesia.

5. Founded by Ardeshir (A.D. 226), who drove out the Parthians. For the first time since the days of the Achaemenians, Persia was governed by native rulers.

6. Tarmukta Stavarak (of Persian origin) has been mentioned earlier. The embroidered Parsi borders made in Gujarat or Mumbai are still renowned for their beauty and are the only decoration on the otherwise plain Parsi saris.

7. Satin weaving is said to have been taught to the Muslims by Chinese prisoners after their defeat by the Muslims at Talas in the eighth century. It has been speculated that Haulgou or Halaku Khan, the conqueror, imported a hundred families of Chinese artists and craftsmen into Persia in A.D. 1226. This seems probable considering the very visible Chinese influence on Persian paintings and textile designs.

8. Similar floral creepers can be seen in Greek architectural decorations in the temple of Hera at Samos, built for the third time in 535-530 B.C. Carved female figures called caryatids served as the pillars of the Greek temple.

9. Findings at Begram in Afghanistan, the site of the summer palace of the Kushan King, Kapisa, show that the Kushan rulers collected toll from the traders.

10. A sun temple was built from the donation given by the guild of silk weavers of Mandasor. This indicates they were wealthy and well regarded in society.

11. Liu, Xinru, *Silk and Religion*, pp. 70, 71.

12. Kucha, in Turfan, was known for its polychrome-patterned silk. A Chinese document dated the mid-fifth century A.D., when Turfan was under Chinese rule and formed one of the sixteen states in North China, refers to 'Kucha polychrome-patterned silk', which was not only popular in China but was also copied there.

13. The history of Islam commences with Mohammad (A.D. 570 to 632). In A.D. 635, Damascus became the capital. Jerusalem was captured in A.D. 637, Egypt in A.D. 641, Persia in A.D. 642, Spain in A.D. 711, Sicily in A.D. 827, and India was invaded in A.D. 997. The main dynasties were the Fatimide Caliphats, the Mamluks of Egypt and Iraq, the Ottomans of Turkey, the Umayyads of Spain, the Safavids of Persia, the Ghaznavids of Khurasan, the Baberids of Kabulistan, the Sultanate and the Mughals of India.

14. Canfield, Robert L., ed. *Turko-Persian in Historical Perspective*, p. 13.

15. Ibid., p. 15.

16. Elliot, H. M. *Account of Masalik*, III, p. 578.

17. Ibn Batuta, *Rehla*, Vol. III, p. 405.

DEVELOPMENT OF PATTERN

There are a range of special patterns which have, over several centuries, become characteristic of Indian textile designs. These motifs and patterns were used not only for their decorative value but also for their strong symbolic connotations, both in mythology and folklore. They played a twofold role – of aesthetic appeal, and as a vehicle for the transmission of an already deeply embedded spiritualised culture. The craftsman himself may not have always been specifically concerned with the numerous symbolic values depicted by the forms he was selecting, but they must have been special for him as a reflection of the various components of daily life.

The trefoil decoration on the shawl of the famous priest sculpture found in Mohenjodaro (Pakistan) of the Indus Valley Civilisation is the earliest example of an Indian textile pattern. This was one of the most popular patterns, and continues to be so till today – in Varanasi it is referred to as the *tinpatia* pattern. The trefoil pattern has an international history, having originated in Mesopotamia, Egypt and Crete, where it was associated with a religious character.[1] Possibly the Mohenjodaro bust was intended to portray a deity or priest, and was therefore adorned with the best material available – brocade.

A study of designs found on the pottery of the Harappan civilisation (3500 B.C.) reveals that certain motifs were popular throughout the later centuries, and can still be found in Indian art, including in textiles. Archaeological findings reveal the significant commercial link between India, Mesopotamia and the Persian Gulf. Fragments of painted pottery excavated at sites in Baluchistan[2] and Afganistan also reveal a similarity in decorative motifs. Some of these, used to decorate pottery, can be found in the textile motifs in the cave paintings at Ajanta, medieval Jain and early Rajasthani miniature paintings and architectural decorations. They are also found in textile patterns, such as the chequer board pattern, the loops with suspended lines, the step and the chevron motifs and the zigzag lines used for border decorations, and the opposed triangles that were popular later in the *phulkari* of the Punjab.

The depiction of stylised deer, antelope, humped bull and tigers, which are seen in south Indian, Paithani and Gujarati fabrics of a later period, was commonly found on the chalcolithic pottery of Iran and Central Asia.[3] Animals in horizontal fringes have also been depicted on pots found in Chandoli and Nevasa[4] and can be compared with the pottery-decoration patterns of Giyan and Bakun in Iran.

Rows of animals (elephants, lions and swans) can be seen in the Hoyesaleshwar temple decorations in Karnataka, and on the walls of the old Vishwanath temple in Varanasi. The Kanjeevaram saris of south India also have similar panels of animal motifs on their elaborate *pallus* (Plate 47, page 68).

Another motif of a man riding an elephant was found on a seal at Maska in Andhra Pradesh. This was a popular Gujarati motif (Plate 58, page 78) used on the *pallus* of Ashavali saris and later in Banaras brocades.

Spots or circles, one of the most widely used motifs of a later period, representing the sun and moon, were popular among people of the Jhukar civilisation (1700 B.C.) in the Indus delta. The pattern has also been found on the Tell-Halaf and Al'ubaid pottery of Iran, in which the spots are with single or multiple loops, both large and small. Other decorative motifs were shapes such as crescents, triangles, six- and four-armed crosses and so forth. Plants and trees were also depicted, which were similar to the Assyrian version of the Tree of Life motif. Peacocks, star-shaped roundels, and stylised birds in U shapes, found on jars, are still used as decorative motifs in Gujarati and Rajasthani fabrics, particularly those of the frontier areas.

It is clear from the historical evidence available, that north and west India, central Asia, Persia, Iraq and Turkey were regions with rich textile-weaving centres. It is significant that the decorative motifs popular in these areas during the pre-historic period continued to be so in later centuries too. Decorative motifs on the pottery fragments excavated from the Persian, Iraqi, and northwestern sites of the Indian subcontinent such as Jhukar, Quetta, Kot Digi, Gumla, Tal-i-Bakum, Susa, Ur, Kish, and Tepe Hissar show a marked similarity with the fragment found at the chalcolithic site in the Deccan (1300-1000 B.C.). Therefore, it is difficult to assign one place as the source of any motif. Certain motifs were, however, more popular in one particular area, and therefore became synonymous with that region.

Archaeologists attribute these motifs to the Aryans, and believe they developed and spread to the areas where the Aryans migrated, and also through trade. An almost similar culture was shared by a vast area comprising west Asia, southern Europe, and a part of northwest India, which was also known for the development of silk brocades during a later period. There is no doubt that these decorative motifs were also used in textiles, as is the case even today.

INDIAN CLASSICAL MOTIFS AND THEIR SYMBOLISM

The Indian weaver predominantly used a wide variety of classical motifs such as the swan (*hamsa*), the lotus (*kamala*), the Tree of Life (*kalpa vriksha*), the Vase of Plenty (*purna kumbha*), the elephant (*hathi*), the lion (*simha*), flowing floral creepers (*lata patra*), peacocks (*mayur*), and many more. These motifs have remained in existence for more than two thousand years. However, new patterns have consistently been introduced,

Facing page

■ Plate: 29
PATKA, 17TH CENTURY. THE LOTUS WAS A POPULAR INDIAN MOTIF USED IN CENTRAL ASIA AND PERSIA.

Preceding page 46

■ Plate: 28
BANARAS YARDAGE FROM THE 19TH-20TH CENTURY SHOWS THE *ARI-JHARI* OR DIAGONALLY STRIPED PATTERN.

■ Plate: 30
BLOUSE, VARANASI,
19TH CENTURY. THE
ANGULAR ZIG-ZAG
PATTERN IS KNOWN AS
TIKONI LAHARIYA.

Below

■ Plate: 31
PURSE, LOOM FINISHED,
GUJARAT, 19TH CENTURY.
ELEPHANTS WITH RIDERS
FLANK A WISH-FULFILLING
TREE.

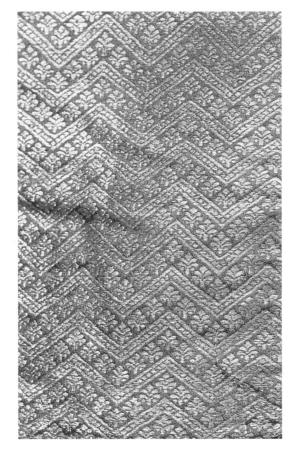

sometimes some of these are even an amalgamation of existing patterns. Such attempts at evolving new designs were particularly noticeable from the tenth century onwards, when patterns were altered to meet the specific demands of the Muslim rulers.

A brief overview is necessary to understand the significance of patterns in Indian textiles, and to become familiar with the multivalent symbolism conveyed by these motifs. A vase of plenty symbolises prosperity and fullness. The tree of life is the wish-fulfilling tree. A lotus is associated with purity and perfection, and is also a symbol of spiritual unfolding and divine creative energy. The elephant symbolises affluence, and is considered to be one of the nine treasures (*nidhi*). The lion denotes power, and the horse symbolises time and speed – as Lord Surya's mount, it is the *ashwin* (harbinger) of dawn in Rigvedic lore. The bull (Nandi) symbolises pleasure, enormous creative faculties, power, strength, and endurance. The swan is associated with wisdom, and is also the symbol of purity. The peacock denotes the seven rays of the sun seen in its feathers. It also symbolises the rainy season. The eagle, called *suparna* (the fair feathered one), signifies power.

A number of geometric patterns, such as squares, diagonal lines, hexagons, octagons, circular forms, or zigzag lines, and so forth were used in borders and for background decoration. Often, floral, animal or bird motifs were also incorporated with these (Plate 32).

Mythical creatures such as winged lions, centaurs, griffins, decorative or ferocious

animals, animals formally in profile or with turned heads, animal and human figures in combat, or represented in roundels, were commonly used motifs. According to Coomaraswamy, 'All that belongs to this phase of art is equally the common inheritance of Europe and Asia; and its various forms as they occur in India or elsewhere at various periods up to the present day are to be regarded as cognates rather than borrowings.'[5] A number of motifs common in Chinese Han silk (Han Dynasty 206 B.C. – A.D. 220) were probably the originals of those used in the fifteenth and sixteenth-century silk brocades of Persian, Sicilian and Indian origin.

In ancient times, interaction between distant civilisations was the prerogative of traders, political envoys and religious missionaries, taking and bringing with them diverse cultural and artistic influences. Indian kings sent envoys to major royal courts in distant lands since the pre-Christian era. Religious missionaries, particularly Buddhist monks, established their centres in various parts of central Asia

■ Plate: 32
YARDAGE, VARANASI, 19TH CENTURY. AN EXAMPLE OF GUJARATI PATTERN ON A BANARAS BROCADE FRAGMENT. THE SILK GROUND IS DIVIDED INTO LARGE SQUARES THAT HAVE PEACOCK *BUTAS*.

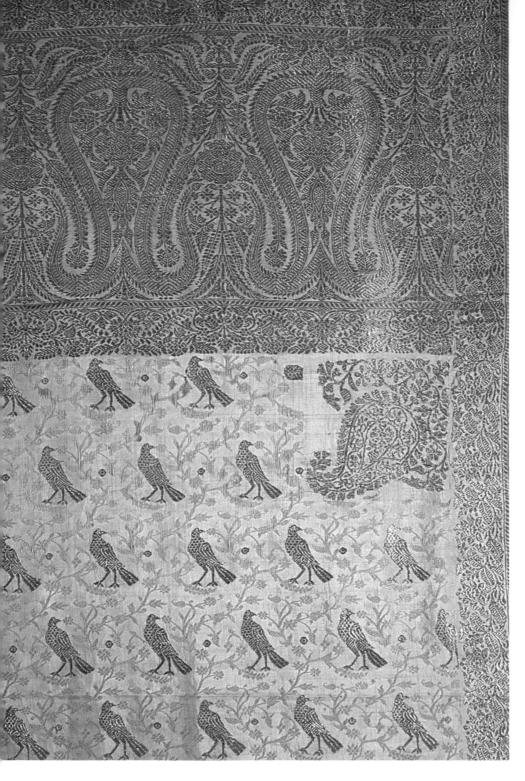

and China, and built monasteries, which they decorated with beautiful brocades. Since India was the birthplace of Buddhism, the motifs on these brocades were Indian, such as the lotus, swan, elephant, lion, bull and the Bodhi tree.

Chinese polychrome silks with foreign designs were produced for both foreign and domestic markets. Those with Indian motifs may have had a religious meaning and were suitable for Buddhist pilgrims or traders, who carried them as gifts westwards to India or central Asia. Apart from these, fine fabrics were made for the Indian market, which were highly valued in the courts of Indian rulers.

From the seventh century A.D., Yang Chou in southern China specialised in making polychrome silk for robes worn by foreigners.[6] This may have been *chincholak*, so popular in ancient Indian royal courts. The Chinese elite, however, had already developed a taste for imported silk, which was mostly Persian. Chinese weavers began copying these patterns (using western technology) for the local market. The weft-faced compound twill with typical Persian animal motifs and roundels became very popular in China.

Such motifs (animals in roundels or squares) were found in brocades made in Paithan (Plate 50, page 71) and Kanchipuram till the eighteenth and nineteenth centuries, and are still popular.

In the absence of any surviving example of ancient Indian textiles, fabric patterns represented on the Ajanta cave paintings of the seventh century give us some idea about the patterns used and appreciated during that period. It is interesting that all the patterns are still in use thirteen hundred years later! This is ample proof of the loyalty of the weavers and their patrons to their tradition, which resulted in the continuity of these patterns – for example, the bull or the swan, arranged between vertical or diagonal stripes, can still be found in the silk brocade saris of Kanchipuram and Tanjore. In Ajanta, a female figure is shown wearing a blouse with circular decorations (similar to the *ashrafi* or gold-coin pattern), and a skirt with purple, green and yellow stripes, similar to the striped *mashru* fabric of later times. Patterns with small flowers and two-coloured squares (chessboard design) are seen, used both as a garment and as furnishing material – bedspreads with the same kind of pattern are still woven in some parts of Gujarat.

In the seventeenth cave, the king of Kashi is shown worshipping a golden swan, and many lengths of fabric are used as curtains. One of them has a green background with diagonal stripes and a floral pattern typical of nineteenth-century Banaras brocades (Plate 28, page 46).

Another motif represented in the first cave resembles the head of an arrow, which may be a stylised form of flying birds – similar patterns can be seen in *mashru* (Plate 13, page 30) fabrics made in Gujarat and Maharashtra till the late nineteenth century.

Facing page

■ Plate: 33
SARI (DETAIL), VARANASI, EARLY 20TH CENTURY. IT HAS A WHITE DAMASCUSED GROUND WITH A GOLD *ZARI* FALCON MOTIF.

References

1. Agrawal, V.S., *Indian Art*, p. 20.
2. Piggot, A., *New Prehistoric Ceramics from Baluchistan*, p. 138.
3. Asthana, Shashi, *History and Archaeology of Indian Contact with Other Countries*, p. 89.
4. Ibid.
5. Coomarswamy, A.K., *History of Indian and Indonesian Art*, 1965.
6. Liu, Xinru, *Silk and Religion*, p. 18.

BROCADE WEAVING

A general definition of brocade is a fabric with a woven pattern which is purely decorative and independent of the structure of the cloth. This is achieved by using extra pattern weft or extra warp, as in the case of *lampas*. The effect resembles embroidery. The term brocade is a derivation from the Latin word *brocare* (to prick), which suggests needle work. Therefore, the brocade-weaving technique is often defined as embroidery weaving or loom embroidery. Although a fabric made of any fibre, such as wool, linen or cotton, can be decorated using this technique, the term brocade is generally restricted to richly designed fabrics woven with silk and gold or silver thread.

RAW MATERIALS

SILK: The basic raw material of many brocades is mainly mulberry silk thread. This was originally imported from China, Persia and central Asia, and later was also brought from Italy. Apart from the inherent beauty of silk brocades, the fact that they were made from non-indigenous materials added to their value. Japanese and Chinese silk threads were renowned for their superior qualities of evenness and lustre, and were, therefore, coveted by weavers.

Mulberry silk, though inferior to the Chinese variety, was found in India in Assam and Bengal. It also grew in Chota Nagpur, Bihar, Punjab and Kashmir. The well-known indigenous varieties of silk are *eri, munga* and *tassar*. A Chinese species of the mulberry silkworm, *Bombyx Textor*, had once been reared in Murshidabad without much success. Though silk was grown here earlier also, Murshidabad became a flourishing silk centre in the eighteenth and nineteenth centuries, encouraged by the British, whose earliest connection with the district was the establishment of a silk factory around A.D. 1652 on the banks of the river Bhagirathi at Kasimbazar. Later a larger one was established in A.D. 1662. The British paid in gold and silver for all kinds of silks, which they bought from the local cultivators.

After their victory at the Battle of Plassey in A.D. 1757, the British gained power in Bengal. Their hold on the silk trade, which previously was in the hands of the French, Dutch and Armenians, increased. Realising its potential, they extended and organised the sericulture industry in a professional way in Bengal. One of the main reasons for this was that the supply of Persian silk to English traders had come to a standstill. In A.D. 1621, negotiations between the Shah of Persia and the company agent regarding the

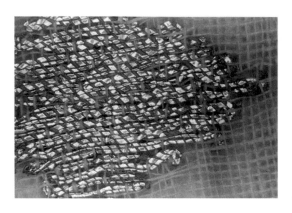

purchase of Persian silk had failed. It was only then that the English merchants began to give serious thought to the possibility of extending sericulture in Bengal, as described by Major J. H. Tull Walsh in his book, *The History of Murshidabad*. To bring it at par with the highly-valued Persian silk, a number of measures were adopted by the East India Company.

Chinese cocoons were imported; filature factories were set up to improve methods of unwinding the silk from the cocoon. Cocoons from other districts of Bengal, Assam, and Orissa also were brought to these factories to unwind the thread. *Tassar* was brought from Assam; its reeling was more difficult than the other varieties.

Most of the silk produced at these factories was exported to France, Italy and England. A small percentage was used by local weavers – these were called *putney, khamra* and *matka*.

By A.D. 1832, the silk industry was no longer a government preserve, and was transferred to private firms, who were mostly British or Armenians. There was a general decline in the industry due to the lack of specialised management in its production and marketing.

Tassar was made from cocoons brought from the jungles of Chybasa and Midnapur. Till the early twentieth century, besides Bengal and Assam, *tassar* coocons were obtained from Chanda, Bilaspur, Sambalpur, and to a lesser extent, from Balaghat, Seoni and Bhandara. In these places, people engaged in the industry were called *dhimars*. *Munga* silk, known for its gloss and quality, was generally used to weave mixed fabrics.

Silk threads were classified according to their structure, texture, characteristics, and laid-down regulations. *Chinya*, the thread made by cutting the silk in staple lengths, followed by spinning and twisting the threads, was also known as spun silk. These threads were used to weave heavy brocades such as *kimkhab*. *Katan,* a thread prepared by twisting a different number of silk filaments according to requirement, gives a firm structure to the background fabric. *Pat* or *pat bana* is a silk thread without a twist, which is used in the weft to achieve a soft and smooth finish, both for heavy and light fabrics.

ZARI is the gold and silver thread, used in Indian brocades. They were produced mainly in Surat and Varanasi. In the late nineteenth century, *zari* was also imported from France.

Zari is generally of two types – *badla* and *kalabattu*. *Badla zari* was made of flattened gold or silver wire, the ancient method of making *zari* from pure metal without any core thread. This accounted for its peculiar stiffness. Sometimes cracks developed in the metal during the process of weaving. This resulted in the loss of its natural lustre and smoothness, and therefore weaving with *badla zari* was difficult and required great skill. Often a touch of *badla* was given to floral motifs to enhance their beauty. This type of *zari* has gone out of favour among contemporary weavers.

The other type of *zari* is *kalabattu*. In this, thin silver or gold wire is wound around silk or cotton, and now even rayon thread. The technique for making *kalabattu* demands that the silver wire pass through a series of holes in an iron plate called a *jantri*. The holes are arranged in decreasing sizes, and the silver wires which go through them are pulled to the required fineness by means of *charkhas* or spinning wheels. The wire is then ready for winding on silk threads. Silver wire is wound around white thread to make silver *zari* called *rupa*. To make gold *zari*, gold is placed around the holes of the *jantri* during the final stages of pulling the wire. The heat generated by the wire as it passes through the *jantri* gives the silver wire a gold coating, which is subsequently wound around yellow thread. It is not uncommon to find a blend of gold and silver *zari* in brocades – the impact is called *Ganga Jamuni*.[1]

DYES: Silk has a remarkable affinity for dyes. In fact, much of its allure lies in its capacity to absorb a wide range of colours and display them so favourably because of its sheen and texture. Before the advent of commercial chemical dyes, natural and vegetable dyes were used. A few examples are the leaves of the indigo plant (*indigofera tinctoria*), turmeric root (*curcuma longa*),

pomegranate skin, *katechu*, lac, iron rust, and a number of flowers, particularly the sunflower and *parijat*. Till the beginning of the twentieth century, both natural and chemical dyes were used. These were imported from Germany, Austria and England. Invented in Europe in 1868, they were called *bukni* in India and were available as powders. Though their colours were brilliant, they were often 'fugitive'. However, they had many advantages such as a large range of colours, low cost, and the simple dyeing process.

Today, in spite of the tentative renewal of interest in vegetable dyes, chemical dyes maintain their dominance and India is a major manufacturer and exporter. Each company has its own shade card with numbers (not names) given to the different shades. The modern weaver is therefore not even familiar with the traditional names of the colours, such as *sultani surkh* (scarlet), *mashi* (grass green), *mungia* (light yellowish green), *lajwardi* (lapis lazuli blue), *motia* (yellowish white), *gandhaki* (sulphur yellow), *kapasi* (pale yellow), *kafuri* (straw coloured), *uda* (purple blue), *kaulai* (deep orange), and so forth. These names are no longer used. Some other popular colours were *pyazi* (light purple pink), *gulabi* (pink), *lal* (red), *badami* (light buff), *karaundiya* (puce), *narangi* (orange), *kesaria* (saffron), *baigani* (violet), *zard* (yellow), *nimbui* (lemon yellow), *kahi* (dark green), *sabz kahi* (light green), *sabz* (green), *asmani* (sky blue), *ferozi* (turquoise blue) and *syah* (midnight blue).

Generally silk is dyed with acid colours, though it has an affinity for direct basic and reactive dyes. Acid colours are best, however,

■ Plate: 36
BORDER FRAGMENT SHOWING
TAPESTRY WEAVE, PAITHAN,
19TH CENTURY. THE
PEACOCK AND THE PARROT,
TWO FAVOURITE MOTIFS OF
WESTERN INDIAN TEXTILES,
ARE REPRESENTED IN A
FLORAL CREEPER.

because they are colour fast and easy to use. Silk is the queen of fibres. The use of reactive dyes enhances its lustre, but this process requires great care and skill. Moreover, the cost factor prevents the common weaver from using them. However, they are adept at dyeing the best quality silks.

WEAVING THE PATTERN

A variety of techniques are used for weaving silk. The plain background is woven with tabby, twill or satin weave. Various methods for creating patterns on plain textiles are used such as brocade, tapestry etc. The tapestry weave was also used in ancient Egyptian (Coptic), Indian (Paithani) and Sassanian textiles. In this weave, warp is stretched on the loom and weft threads of different colours are woven into it, not across the whole width of the warp, but each one only in the areas where its colour is required to form the pattern. Pattern formation depends on the capability of the weaver (as in embroidery); the most skilled weavers can produce patterns of any size and type, even with intricate details.

As already mentioned, in a brocade weave extra weft threads of different coloured silk or *zari* are woven into the basic fabrics as required, and only in the areas where they are to form a pattern. In this kind of weave,

unlike in a tapestry weave, there is also a main weft thread which runs from selvage to selvage, forming a woven foundation for the pattern weft. The different techniques of making a pattern are named after the way the shuttle of extra weft yarn is manoeuvred through the shades of warp yarn. The most beautiful and intricate patternmaking technique, it is called *kadwa* or embroidered. It requires as many weft shuttles of different coloured silk as are needed to form the pattern. Each pattern (*buta*) appearing on the fabric has its own set of shuttles, which are allowed to float under the surface when not required, this is also called *meenakari* or enamelling. Some of the terms used for this technique in Varanasi are *guddi meena* (when the *meena* work is used only for the inner core of the *buti*), *tipaki meena* (a very fine small dot made with coloured silk), and *rang badal meena* (if three or four colours are used in a single flower). The *meenakari* technique is beautifully represented in Gujarati (Plate 64, page 85) and Paithani (Plate 2, page 12) brocades, where the background of the pattern area is woven with gold or silver *zari,* on which patterns are highlighted with coloured silk. In Varanasi, the weaving style is just the opposite – the background is of silk, and *zari* is used to make the pattern (Plate 95, page 110). Another weaving technique called *Urtu* (which probably originated in the ancient west Asian textile weaving region called Urartu), is the specialty of Banaras brocade weavers, and is also referred to as *Banarasi Hunar* (art). In this, the pattern weft is manipulated by using multiple weave (plain, satin, twill) and thus a different ground pattern is achieved in a

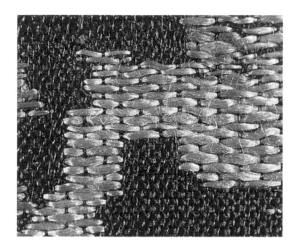

■ Plate: 37
LAMPAS TECHNIQUE, ASSAM.

single pattern. *Fekwa* is the throwing of the pattern weft shuttle fully across the warp and appearing on the surface only in the space occupied by the pattern. This method is easier, but the fabric is messier on the reverse side. *Katraua* or cutwork is the same as *fekwa*, except that the extra weft threads running on the reverse between the two patterns are cut away so that the pattern is neater on the obverse side. This method is cheaper and quicker and used mostly these days.

Lampas, an ancient technique of creating pattern on fabric earlier than brocade and mostly used in China, central Asia and northeast India (Assam). Two warps are used, one to make the background, and the other to bind the pattern weft. The pattern weft is thrown across, and the warp appears on the surface according to the requirement of the pattern. In Varanasi, *lampas* were made in the Badi Bazar area. The fabrics made with the *lampas* weave were *sangi* and *galta,* which were of mixed material, i.e., cotton and silk.

Top, left

■ Plate: 38
BROCADE WEAVE, TURKEY.

Top, right

■ Plate: 39
BROCADE WEAVE, INDIA,
19TH CENTURY.

Below

■ Plate: 40
URTU TECHNIQUE, VARANASI,
LATE 19TH CENTURY.

Facing page

■ Plate: 41, *right*
REVERSE OF BROCADE WEAVE,
PERSIA, 18TH CENTURY.

Left:
OBVERSE OF THE SAME
WEAVE.

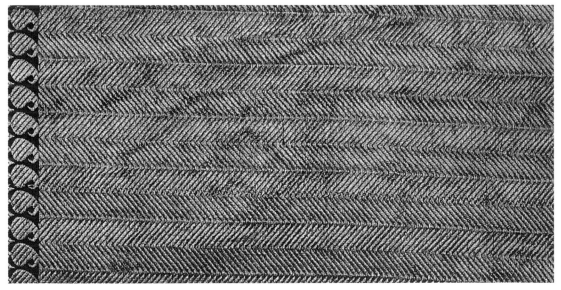

In *sangi,* two warps of two different colours, usually white and blue *katan* silk, were used. Cotton weft was woven to obtain a wavy pattern. It was a popular fabric made in many weaving centres, especially in Azamgarh Mau and Badi Bazar in Varanasi. The process of weaving *sangi* was time-consuming and tedious, and profits were not large, so it gradually fell out of favour.[2] *Galta* was woven with satin weave using *katan* silk. It had a double warp, one above and one below. The lower warp was woven tight, and the upper one loosely, which created a self-patterned surface.

Satin weave was introduced first in Gujarat and then in Varanasi during the late nineteenth or the beginning of the twentieth century. Damask weaving was also introduced around the same time, probably brought either by Gujarati weavers from Surat, or weavers who had migrated from Lahore, as Lahore was known for its satin damask material. Damask weaving was called *vasket* weaving in Varanasi because this fabric was primarily used for making European-style waistcoats called *vasket* in the local language.

FABRIC TYPES

Brocade fabrics may be classified into two general types: loom-finished and yardage. Brocades woven as yardage are versatile in their usage. While most often used as dress material, they are also used as upholstery, curtains, and book covers. The *choga* (a long, loose man's coat) was made from yardage, but was also woven on the loom according to the shape of the garment, particularly in the nineteenth and early twentieth centuries. Loom-finished fabrics are saris, *odhnis, patkas,* caps, *pankhas, sanjabs (sinjab),* curtains, *pichwais, pithias,* and so forth.

The best-known brocade fabrics were the **KAMKHWAB OR KINKHAB** (Plates 2, 6, 7; pages 12, 20, 23) Varanasi, Ahmedabad and Surat were centres which specialised in weaving this fabric, which is known worldwide. Its splendour and elegance, combined with its cost, gave it its name, which means 'something a person cannot dream of if he has not seen it,' (*kam:* little, scarcely; *khwab:* dream), or 'a fabric which is seldom or rarely seen in a dream', or 'the golden (*kin*) dream (*khwab*)'. *Kin* means golden in Chinese. Its speciality is such a profuse use of gold and silver thread that sometimes the silk background is hardly visible. It is used mainly to make heavy ceremonial robes, hangings, and furnishings. A few well known varieties are:

ALFI: This is a kind of patterned *zari* brocade, used as dress material, especially for a tight-fitting long coat, a *sherwani.* It is an expensive and fashionable fabric, used to make ceremonial outfits – the gold or silver *zari butis* are outlined with single or double-coloured thread, and the pattern is called *meenakari* (enamelling). In *alfi,* only the outline of the pattern is made with coloured silk; the inner work is always either in silver or gold thread. Double-coloured outlined *alfi* is more expensive because it needed more skill and time in weaving. It is a speciality of Varanasi.

Facing page

■ Plate: 42
ALFI BROCADE, *SHERWANI* OR LONG GENTS COAT, VARANASI, LATE 19TH CENTURY. THE SATIN GROUND IS DENSELY COVERED WITH A FINE FLORAL PATTERN.

TASHI: This is a variety of *kinkhwab* which has the ground worked with an extra warp of gold *badla zari* and the pattern created with an extra weft of silver *badla zari* or vice versa. Another kind is called *meenatashi,* in which patterns are woven either with gold or silver, combined with coloured threads, on a golden or silver background. In the *tash badla* variety, *badla* (flat wire) is used as extra weft on silk warp. These fabrics were used to make wedding robes (*jama*), trappings, hangings, and so forth. They were sold by their weight, and not by the yard. Sometimes *kalabattu* was also used with *badla* to form a pattern.

POT THAN OR BAFTA: These are called *katan* brocades too. In them the silk background is patterned with silk thread or *zari*, the material is lighter and is used to make expensive garments and saris.

HIMRU OR AMRU: These are woven like *kinkhwabs,* but without the use of *kalabattu* (*zari*). The pattern is woven using silk thread on silk.

MASHRU: This is a mixed fabric with a woven striped or zigzag pattern. The warp and weft used were of two different materials (silk and cotton, cotton and linen, silk and wool or wool and cotton) in different colours. It was used mostly for lower garments (such as trousers), the lining of the heavy brocade garments or as furnishing. *Gulbadan,* the literal meaning of it is flower-like body, was a known variety of *mashru* (cotton and silk) popular till the late nineteenth century. *Sangi, Galta,* and *Ilaycha*

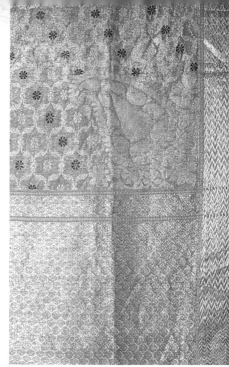

(mentioned earlier) were types of *mashru*, too. They were popular since ancient times and made at almost all weaving centres. Since Islam did not allow men to wear pure silk, *mashru* (literally meaning permitted) became popular among Muslims.

TISSUE: A thin transparent lightweight material used mainly for turbans (*safas*), veils, *dupatta*s (long scarves) and saris. However, sometimes it is also used as dress material. Tissue or *tarbana* is made of single silk warp and single gold weft.

***KORA* SILK**: The warp and weft of this material is made of pure raw silk with designs made with extra cotton weft. It is used as dress material and saris.

Left

■ Plate: 44
MASHRU, YARDAGE, 19TH CENTURY, GUJARAT.

Right

■ Plate: 45
SARI, VARANASI, 19TH CENTURY. SILK GAUZE SARI WOVEN WITH THE *TASHI* TECHNIQUE. *TASHI* WAS PROBABLY THE ANCIENT GOLD OR SILVER CLOTH MADE IN INDIA, CHINA, AND TIBET.

Facing page

■ Plate: 43
HIMRU, YARDAGE, GUJARAT, 18TH CENTURY. BUNCH OF FLOWERS COMING OUT OF A VASE ON A SATIN GROUND - A FAVOURITE MUGHAL MOTIF.

References

1. Ganga and Jamuna are two of north India's major rivers. The term *Ganga Jamuni* is frequently used in Varanasi to describe the meeting of two objects which are different in nature. Here the phrase implies the meeting of the white waters of the Ganga (silver) and the darker waters of the Jamuna (gold).
2. Abu Sardar, belonging to an old *sangi*- and *galta*-weaving family of Badi Bazar, remembers a phrase which was used among the *sangi* weavers '*Sangi Bine Tangi Awe, Ladikan Jaye Naniaure*' meaning the *sangi* weaver cannot feed his family and is obliged to send the children away to the house of their maternal grandparents. The phrase expresses the unrewarding and unremitting hardship involved in *sangi*- or *galta*-weaving, and the reason why it came to an end. In its time, it was used to make *sherwanis*, the tight-fitting long mens' coat in vogue in the early twentieth century.

SOUTHERN AND WESTERN INDIAN BROCADES

The brocade-weaving centres of India developed in and around the capitals of kingdoms or holy cities because of the demand for expensive fabrics by the royal families and temples. Rich merchants of the trading ports or centres also contributed to the development of these fabrics. Besides trading in the finished product, they advanced money to the weavers to buy the costly raw materials, i.e., silk and *zari*.

The ancient centres were situated mainly in Gujarat, Malwa and south India. It is mentioned in ancient literature that Mandasor (western Malwa) and Lat Desh (south Gujarat) were renowned for their fine and expensive fabrics (particularly during the Gupta period, fourth to sixth centuries A.D.). The traders and weavers were prosperous enough to give donations and build a sun temple. The Hindu dynasties of the period, the Rashtrakutas, Chalukyas, Vakatakas, Pallavas and Cholas were known for their prosperity and patronage of art and culture. Many famous centres such as Paithan, Surat, Ahmedabad, Patan, Chanderi, Mandasor, Kanchi, Trichinapally and Tanjore made fabrics for the royal courts, but many disintegrated after the withdrawal of royal patronage, and the weavers migrated to other centres mainly around new royal capitals, religious or trade centres. These migrant weavers created new centres and also brought new techniques and designs to some of the existing centres such as Varanasi, Murshidabad and others. While assimilating new ideas, they also retained their traditions, which often betrayed their place of origin. Delhi, Agra, Lahore, Fatehpur Sikri, Lucknow (Jalalpura), Mau, Azamgarh, Varanasi and Murshidabad were centres in north India which developed mainly because of the migration of weavers from established silk-weaving centres.

SOUTHERN OR DECCANI BROCADES

The *Manasollasa*, composed in A.D. 1130-31 by the Chalukya king Bhulokamalla Someshwara, is one of the texts which refers to the excellent textiles of Thondai-mandalam. It has descriptions of saris variegated by lines in different colours, with five colours used in the *pallu*.[1] Spiral circular patterns, squares and dots were also used, which match the designs on garments seen in the Ajanta cave paintings. The square chequered pattern seen on pottery from

■ Plate: 47
TEMPLE SARI, 19TH CENTURY,
TANJAUR/KANCHIPURAM.
THE MOTIFS SHOW MANY
ANCIENT TRADITIONS: THE
GROUND IS COVERED WITH
ROUNDELS AND THE *PALLU*
HAS THE STANDING BULL
AND GALLOPING HORSE
MOTIFS IN HORIZONTAL
BANDS SIMILAR TO THE
ARCHITECTURAL DECORATION
OF SOUTHERN TEMPLES.

Preceding page 66

■ Plate: 46
GENTS' PYJAMA, LATE 19TH
CENTURY, GUJARAT. FLOWER
BUTIS ARE ARRANGED IN
GOLDEN *BADRUM ZAL*; THE
BUTIS ARE MADE IN *GANGA-
JAMUNI ZARI*.

panchrangi (horizontal bands in five colours), or *muthuchir* (horizontal lines of dots and dashes resembling pearls).[3] The surface of the textile was textured with twill weave to give it a rich look.[4]

Kanchipuram was a famous brocade-weaving centre in south India from ancient times. This temple town, the abode of Goddess Kamakshi, was the capital of the Thondaimandalam region. It was the capital of the Pallava kings (seventh century A.D.) and was visited by the Chinese pilgrim Hiuen Tsang. The town was also the capital of the ruling dynasties of the Cholas (eleventh century) and the Rayas of Vijaynagar (fifteenth century). Kanchipuram's silk-weaving trade prospered because of royal patronage, the temple of Kamakshi, and the river Polar (which facilitated trade while its water was supposed to give the dyed silks of the region their characteristic lustre). Pulicut, the main sea port until 1864, was a part of the Vijaynagar kingdom. Durate Barbosa, a Portuguese traveller who visited Vijaynagar in A.D. 1516, described the city as a 'seat of active commerce' saying, 'diamonds and rubies from Pegu (Burma), silks from China and Alexandria [came there] . . . .' According to him, the Raya King wore a coat of *Zaitunia*, a Chinese brocade imported from the Chinese port of Zaytun.

It is said that the Kanchi silk-weaving tradition goes back to the time of the Pattu Saliyar silk weavers' migration to Kanchipuram, when the maritime city of Kaveripoompattinam was submerged in the sea in the second century A.D. However, the Madras census report of 1891 attributed the

Amri and Ur was used widely in southern Indian fabrics. It might also have been inspired by the chess board, as the game is supposed to have originated in south India. Edgar Thurston, writing about these textiles in A.D. 1899, mentions that 'one cloth with a chequered pattern is fancifully called High Court *papli*, as the squares of alternating colours resemble the flooring tiles in the corridors of the Madras High Court.'

Besides checks and stripes of different widths, other background patterns were *malligai mogu* (jasmine buds), *pavun* (gold coins),[2] stars, *kamala* (lotus flowers), origin of the craft to the migration of weavers at the invitation of the Chola King Raj Raja I (A.D. 985-1014). This seems more probable and would explain the similarity in the motifs of south Indian brocades and those of Gujarat and Paithan (from where the weavers may have come). The craft further developed due to the migration of the weaving communities of the Devangas and the Saligars during the reign of the Emperor Krishna Deva Raya of Vijaynagar (A.D. 1509-1529), who was known as a great patron of the arts.[5]

According to some records, the Kanchi silk-weaving tradition is believed to have begun only around the late eighteenth century. But this was a revival because the city was burnt down by the French in A.D. 1757 after a political defeat, and the silk-weaving craft was destroyed too. It was rehabilitated again, both by the local weavers and by those who had migrated from Gujarat (following repeated natural disasters in their homeland, such as famine and drought).[6]

The traditional saris or *dupattas* of Kanchi had a fine cotton 'ground' with a silk and *zari* border and *pallu*. The patterns on Kanchipuram saris, (Tanjore, Kumbakonam, Trichinapally and Salem being the other silk-weaving centres) prove that the continuity of designs is more than two thousand years old. These fabrics were called *Kanchivani*. They displayed a predominance of bird and animal motifs, and the rich gold-brocaded *pallus* (Plate 47, page 68) and borders had patterns of rows of deer, peacocks, galloping horses, bulls, elephants, parrots, swans and other birds, and even mythical animals – one such

creature was the *yali* with a lion's head and a bird's body; another was a combination of a swan and peacock, which is still a major decorative motif in south Indian designs (often the tail of a peacock takes the form of a decorative *carrie)*. The double-headed eagle, an ancient Mesopotamian motif and the royal emblem of Byzantine kings, was also the royal insignia of the Mysore state and became a popular south Indian motif called *ganda bherunda*. The double-headed eagle was referred to as *dvishirshni suparni* and also as *ubhayatah shirshni* in Vedic literature.[7] It was also a popular ancient Egyption motif symbolising power. It is possible that the pattern was brought to south India from west Asia, probably by traders. Some borders have bead motifs of *rudraksh*[8] (*rudraksham*), *kodivisiri* (floral motifs contained within two lines), and diamond patterns. The *mayilkan* (peacock's eye) and *kuyilkan* (nightingale's eye) designs are adaptations from the Salem tradition called *bulbul chashma* in Varanasi (Plate 8, page 24). Fabrics made at the southern centres were coveted gifts for the ladies of northern India, as is mentioned in two Rajasthani composition of the seventeenth century, *Kapada Chintani* and *Kapada Kutuhal,* written in Braj Bhasha.[9] The sari and *dupatta* from Kanchipuram are mentioned as Dakhani Cheer or the fabrics from south. '*Kanchuki of the charming Machhipatam*' is the short blouse made of the fabric from Masulipattam, which can also be the term used for the imported fabrics (Chinese or European) marketed from this trade port.

Most south Indian temples had their own weavers[10] who were given land and

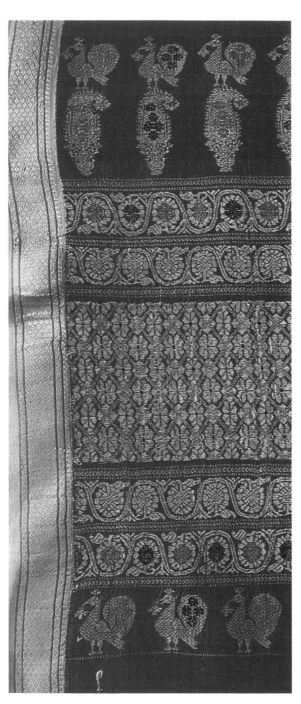

■ Plate: 48, *top*
NINE-YARD SARI, 19TH
CENTURY, PAITHAN/
CHANDERI. THE *PALLU*
WOVEN IN TAPESTRY WEAVE
IS DIVIDED INTO PATTERNED
PANELS. THE MAIN PANEL
HAS SEVEN FLOWER *BUTAS*
WHILE THE NARROW PANEL
HAS TEN SMALLER ONES.

■ Plate: 49, *right*
SARI, 20TH CENTURY,
AURANGABAD/NAGPUR. SUCH
NINE-YARD SARIS WERE
WOVEN FOR THE RICH
FAMILIES OF MAHARASHTRA;
THEIR *PALLU* HAD PANELS
OF DIFFERENT PATTERNS.

houses within the temple town. They wove temple flags, material for decorating chariots, furnishing fabrics and wall hangings depicting figures from the Hindu epics and the *Puranas*. Usually nine-yard saris for the deity or the royal ladies (who wore them for special ceremonies) were woven by this exclusive class of weavers. Dark colours like red, purple, orange, yellow, green and blue predominated in south Indian fabrics.

Adoni in Bellar district (Karnataka), situated at the *doab* (confluence) of the Krishna and Tungabhadra rivers, was an ancient town founded in 1200 B.C. It passed from the Vijaynagar dynasty in A.D. 1564 to the Adil Shahi dynasty of Bijapur, and in A.D. 1670 to the Mughals. In spite of these changes, it remained a raw silk-producing area and weaving was the chief occupation of its people. Fabrics from Adoni were popular locally, and were exported as well.

Paithan, located on the northern bank of the Godavari river (near modern-day Aurangabad in Maharashtra), is one of the oldest cities in the Deccan region. It is mentioned in the *Mahabharata* and in the inscriptions at Pitalkhora near Chalisgaon (dated second century B.C.), which refers to the king and the rich merchants of Pratishtan (Paithan).[11] Aurangabad (near the famous Ajanta caves) was also an important centre in this region.

Paithan, a centre of ancient Dravidian culture, was praised for its wealth and prosperity by ancient historians and travellers from the West, such as Arrian, Pliny, Ptolemy, and others. The city was

■ Plate: 50
END PANEL, *PATKA*, CHANDERI/PAITHAN, 17TH CENTURY. THE MEDALLION SHOWS AN ANIMAL COMBAT SCENE. ROUNDELS WITH ANIMAL, BIRD OR FLORAL MOTIFS ARE AN ANCIENT STYLE.

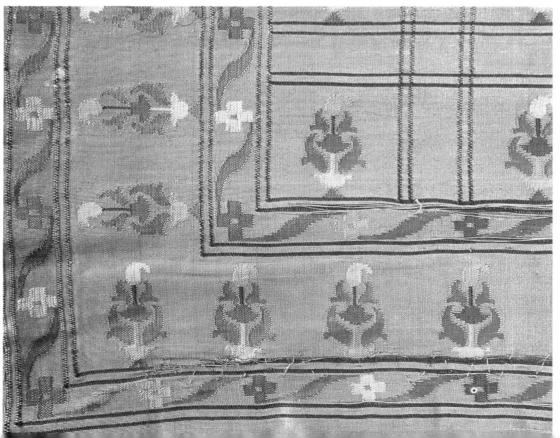

■ Plate: 51
END PIECE OF *PATKA* OR TURBAN, 18TH CENTURY, CHANDERI. THE SILK GAUZE GROUND IS DIVIDED INTO SQUARES WITH A FLORAL PATTERN INSIDE A POPULAR INDIAN PATTERN SEEN IN THE CLOTH DESIGN OF THE WESTERN JAIN PAINTINGS DATED 1280 AND COTTON GUJARATI FRAGMENTS OF THE SAME PERIOD FOUND AT FOSTAT (EGYPT).

71

■ Plate: 52
CHOWKORA, CHANDERI/
GUJARAT, MID-19TH
CENTURY. THE SQUARE VEIL
HAS THE WORDS *SAHEB
KUNWAR BAI SAHEB* WOVEN
INSIDE EACH ROUNDER IN
THE DEVANAGRI SCRIPT
WHICH CAN BE READ FROM
THE REVERSE SIDE. THE
BORDER IS TUCKED
SEPARATELY.

72

noted for its exports through Barugaza (*Brigukachcha,* in Sanskrit*)*, which is modern Bharuch. Its textiles, beads and jewellery were sold at high prices in the markets of Greece, Rome and Egypt. The tapestry weave used in ancient Egypt and Paithan was the oldest technique of weaving textile decorations, which could be used on very fine fabrics, to produce intricate and rich patterns. In the second century A.D., Persian and Sassanian workshops also produced such textiles, which were used mainly to make ceremonial garments.

Rich fabrics made on eastern looms were in great demand in western royal courts and churches. Early Greek writers refer to sumptuously patterned fabrics, used in temple rituals or as the garments of heroes. Euripides speaks of sacred tapestries woven with patterns of heavenly figures, such as the sun driving his horses, with stars scattered on the background, and so on. Another richly patterned fabric described by the Greek writer Homer in the *Odyssey* is the dress of his hero Ulysses, which is one of the earliest depictions of a hunting scene pattern or *shikargah*. 'The purple ground has a pattern of fighting hounds and spotted fawns. They pant and struggle in the moving gold'[12] – the 'moving gold' can be the golden background on which a pattern is woven with different coloured silks. Similar patterns were woven in Paithan. A seventeenth-century sample in the collection of the National Museum in New Delhi depicts rather similar combat scenes, enclosed in a medallion (Plate 50, page 71). The rows of small *carrie butis* on the background edge of the *pallu* can be traced

to the nineteenth and early twentieth century Banarasi work of Madanpura.[13]

The Paithani weave is subtle yet rich. It is known for its closely woven golden fabric, which shines like a mirror. This is its distinguishing mark. In the shimmering gold background, various patterns (of *butas,* the tree of life, stylised birds, curving floral borders, and so forth, worked in red, green, purple and pink) glow like jewels.

Some of the oldest fragments of Paithani weave show a rather narrow elongated stylised *buta,* revealing Persian influence. A *buta* with twin leaves, a flower blossom and bud is a common motif (Plate 1, page 8). Later, larger and more complex *butas* were made, based on Persian prototypes commonly used in Mughal *patkas* and Kashmiri shawls.

Chanderi,[14] near Gwalior in central India, was an ancient town in the Malwa region, famous for its exquisite textiles. In A.D. 1586, it was captured by the Bundelas, and the area came to be known as Bundelkhand. It was famous for its distinctive culture, art and literature. The Bundelkhandis wore their own style of *chogas* and turbans. Gold and silver *zari*-patterned fine cotton and silk turbans, sashes, *dupattas* and saris woven in Chanderi were supplied to the Bundelas and the neighbouring courts of Rajasthan, Gujarat,[15] Maharashtra, and the Mughals. The patterns were similar to those made at other central Indian centres, for example, those in Chanda district. Possibly the weavers of these smaller centres had migrated to Chanderi to seek royal patronage. The cotton 'ground' of these

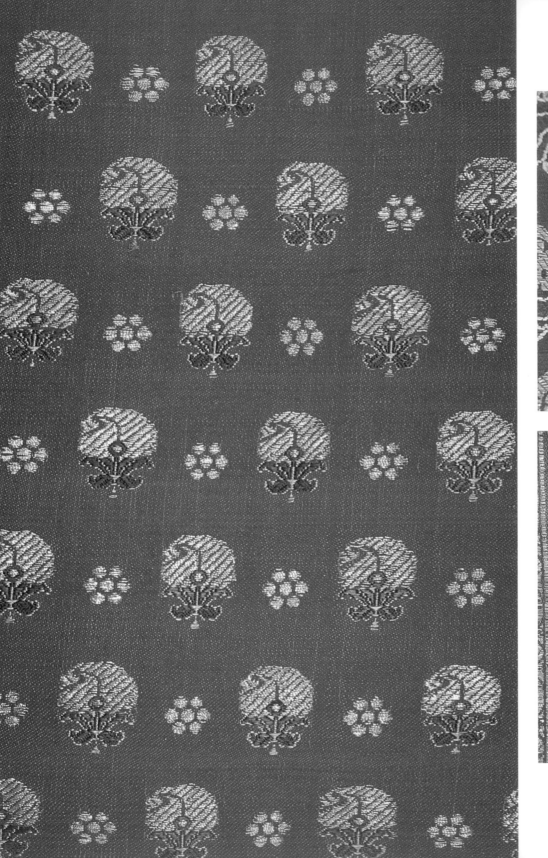

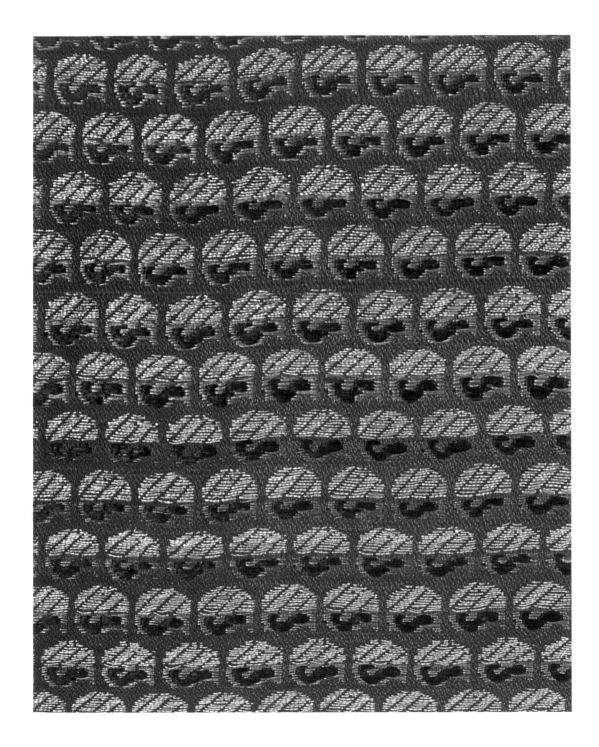

■ Plates: 53, 54, 55, 56
YARDAGE, SILK FRAGMENT,
19TH CENTURY. THERE IS
A GROUP OF BROCADES
WHICH STYLISTICALLY
FALLS IN THE SAME
CATEGORY. SMALL *BUTIS* OR
FLORAL STRIPES ARE MADE
ON DARK COLOURED
GROUND. THE UPPER PART
IS IN GOLD OR SILVER AND
THE BASE IS MADE WITH
FLOSS SILK. SOME MIGHT
HAVE BEEN WOVEN AT
CENTRES IN VIDARBHA,
GUJARAT, TANJAUR OR
TRICHINAPALLY.

fabrics was of unusual fineness and delicacy; it was usually white though colours were used too and had silk and *zari* borders of unsurpassed beauty. Some courtiers in Mughal paintings, particularly in the durbar (court) scene at Shahjahan's court in the *Padshah Namah,*[16] are shown wearing *patkas* with a white 'ground' and multicoloured jewel-like decorations on the gold borders. This may have been a Chanderi fabric, though such material was also woven at Burhanpur, another Deccani centre.

A muslin and gold *zari* sari in the collection of the Museum of Fine Arts, Boston is described in the museum bulletin[17] as belonging to a group of textiles of special beauty. The 'ground' pattern, apart from the double border, represents a *hansa* (swan or goose) in a gold rectangular trellis on a dark green background. The fabric is dated the late seventeenth or early eighteenth century. Similar pieces were made with a peacock or a flower as the central motif inside the trellis in Chanderi (Plates 5, 32; pages 18, 51).[18]

Intricate floral creepers were woven on borders. *Pallus* usually had floral *butas* arranged in horizontal bands. These borders and *pallus* were woven on a solid gold *zari* ground, and patterns were inlaid in brilliant coloured silk threads using the double interlock technique. The pattern looked like jewels worked into the rich gold ground which, as said earlier, looked almost like enamelling on fabric (Plates 2, 36; pages 12, 58). They formed a beautiful contrast with the light texture and light-coloured (mostly white) body, which was either of fine cotton or silk with fine checks. They were woven separately too, and were attached to *saris*, *dupattas*, tray covers or ceremonial square material, and so forth (Plate 52).

A small *chaukora* (square fabric) in the Bharat Kala Bhavan collection has a red cotton background decorated with inscribed medallions. The inscription says: *Saheb Kunwar Baiji Saheb* (an honourable title for a royal lady) in Devanagari script. A broad gold-worked border is attached around it. A similar piece in the Lalbhai collection in Ahmedabad indicates that these were ceremonial pieces, used by certain members of the royal family. The background material was woven as yardage, cut to the required size, and the border was attached to it.

Although tapestry weave was used in both the centres, the difference between the two was that while the Paithani weave was known for its compactness and density, which imparted an extra brilliance and angular appearance to the pattern, the Chanderi weave was comparatively loose, giving it a roundish, and hence a more natural look.[19]

OTHER DECCANI AND CENTRAL INDIAN CENTRES

The continuation of the Paithani style can be seen in Burhanpur brocades. Burhanpur was a province in central India, founded by Nasir Khan in A.D. 1400 during the Farukhi dynasty of Khandesh, and named after the famous Shaikh Burhan-ud-din of Daulatabad.[20] In the *Ain-i-Akbari*, (Akbar's biography by Abul Fazl) Burhanpur is mentioned as a 'large city with many gardens, inhabited by people of all nations and abounding with handicraftsmen.' Similarly, it is mentioned in the *Tuzuk-i-Jahangiri* as a centre from which beautiful textiles were presented to the Mughal Emperor Jahangir (A.D. 1605-1628). Burhanpur muslins, silks and gold brocades were known for their beauty and exquisite weaving. The turbans, *feta* (sashes), saris and *dupattas,* with a pattern format somewhat similar to those of Paithan, were made here, i.e. the plain fine fabric background had narrow gold borders and *pallu* decorated with floral motifs, with a Persian influence. Besides the traditional indigenous light-weight fabrics, heavy Persian-style silk brocades were made here too, probably by Persian weavers working under royal patronage. Burhanpur's geographical position made it a coveted city. It served as an entrepot for trade between Malwa and the Deccan (north and south India) and was therefore an important trading centre during the Mughal period. The Mughals gave importance to the city by sending high-profile governors there. Sir Thomas Roe visited it in A.D. 1614 and went to pay his respects to the governor, Prince Parwez, the son of Jahangir.

In A.D. 1654, the famous French traveller Jean-Baptiste Tavernier visited Burhanpur. Describing the city, he writes, 'There is great trade in the city. There is made a prodigious quantity of calicos (muslin), very clear and white, which are transported into Persia, Turkey, Muscovia, Poland, Arabia, and to grand Cairo and other places.' A variety of textiles were also imported from Persia, Turkey and Central Asia. *Patkas*, fine satin damask dress material, heavy silk and gold-

Facing page

■ Plate: 57
GHARCHOLA SARI, GUJARAT, 19TH CENTURY. FLORAL *BUTAS* ON THE PANEL CAN BE COMPARED WITH THE PERSIAN EXAMPLE ON PLATE 41 (OBVERSE, SEE PAGE 61).

brocaded furnishing material, carpets, and European velvets were the chief Indian imports. It is possible that many textiles from different Indian weaving centres, brought to Burhanpur for trade, came to be known as Burhanpur textiles, though they were actually made elsewhere.[21] The fall of the Mughal empire, and that of the local government, affected the trade and craft in the city. Until the late nineteenth century, the fabric industry was confined to the manufacture of cotton and silk interwoven with gold-plated silver thread, woven in the city. (The purity of these was always tested by English inspectors, probably because they were exported).

Ahmadnagar[22] was another Deccan centre which produced silk and *zari* fabrics. Saris woven there till the late nineteenth century had a high reputation and dealers flocked from neighbouring states and the Nizam's domain to buy them.

Yeola in Nasik district (in Maharashtra) was known for its silk and gold brocades. Gold thread was produced there. Arni in the north Arcot district of Tamil Nadu made *mashru*, which was worn by the elite. This was also exported to other places, including Mysore, and was sold at high prices. Maheshwara, in Madhya Pradesh, was famous for its fine Maheshwari saris with *zari*-decorated borders and *pallus*.

There were many small towns in the Berar district[23] known in their time for their unique textiles, which are no longer weaving centres. Some examples are Chanda, bordered by the Narmada river in the south and Wanganga in the east, which was the capital of the Gonda kings (fifteenth century),[24] and Bhandak, a village near Chanda, which was probably the capital of the old Hindu kingdom of Vakataka (third to fifth centuries A.D.). Both were known for their silk and cotton saris and *dupattas*, which had rich silk borders and *pallus*. Garhcharoli, a small town in Chanda district, was also known for its cotton and silk *dupattas* and saris – originally they were of indigenous *tassar* silk and, as the name suggests, this was probably the home of the famous Gharchola saris of Gujarat (Plate 57), known for their typical pattern of squares with motifs of auspicious symbols, such as elephants, peacocks, swans, lotus flowers, or the vase of plenty inside the trellis, woven with gold and silver *zari* on a cotton or silk ground, as mentioned earlier. Later *mashru* was also woven at Chanda. Ellichpur and Akola in Berar district were also known for their unique textiles. A type of *mashru* fabric called *ellaicha* was probably made there. It is mentioned in the *Imperial Gazetteer* of A.D. 1885 that 'the Telinga weavers turned out cloths of coloured pattern in very good taste.' Nagpur in Vidharbha was known for its finely woven cotton turbans with broad fringes of gold and its saris, generally of plain cotton, with handsome silk borders and *pallus*.[25]

It is also probable that the textiles produced in these smaller towns were traded from Gujarat, and hence came to be known as Gujarati fabrics, though they were made elsewhere. The Gharchola saris became famous as Gujarati wedding saris, but may have been woven at Garhcharoli in Chanda district, or by the weavers from Garhcharoli who may have migrated to

Facing page

■ Plate: 58
SARI, GUJARAT, 1850 A.D. THE ASHAVALI SARI HAS A SATIN SILK GROUND WITH ROSE *BUTIS* IN GOLD *ZARI*. THE MINUTE DETAILS OF THE MOTIFS ON THE *PALLU* ARE NOTEWORTHY.

Gujarat (similar motifs were also woven at Paithan, Chanderi, Tanjore, Kanchipuram and Varanasi).

GUJARATI BROCADES

As mentioned earlier, Gujarat was a renowned brocade-weaving centre since the ancient period. Historical records of the thirteenth century throw more light on the fine textiles produced in Bharuch and Cambay. Referred to as *baroji* and *kambayati* by the thirteenth century Venetian traveller Marco Polo and the Arab chronicler Al Newayri, they are described as outstanding varieties of textiles[26]. They may have been referring to brocades and furnishing material, which were popular in the courts of Indian rulers. Marco Polo (A.D. 1271-95) also described 'beautiful mats in red and blue leather, exquisitely inlaid with gold and silver wire'.[27] It is possible that the same patterns were copied for the brocade furnishing material, for which Surat was famous (Plates 64, 77; pages 85, 96).

Ahmed Shah founded Ahmedabad in A.D. 1412 on the site of the old city of Ashaval. The Ashavali saris of Ahmedabad, known for their beautiful brocade borders and *pallus*, take their name from the ancient town, which probably was known for making such fabrics. This validates the city's association with the finest quality of silk and gold fabrics even prior to the fifteenth century. Ahmedabad,[28] Surat, Bharuch, Patan and Baroda were the main weaving centres. The decorative motifs of the Gujarati architectural masterpieces, which was the outcome of the blending of Sarcenic

79

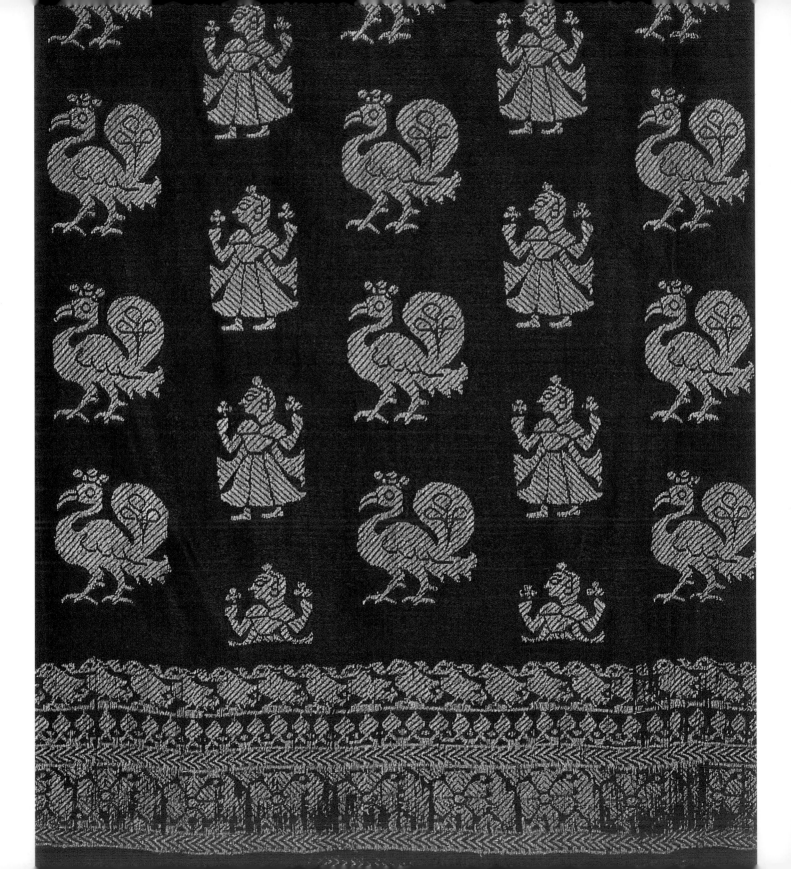

■ Plate: 60
YARDAGE, MID-20TH
CENTURY, VARANASI. THE
FEMALE HOLDING A FLAG
MAY REPRESENT THE
FREEDOM STRUGGLE OR
BHARAT MATA. THE
INFLUENCE OF GUJARATI
MOTIFS IS APPARENT.

Facing page

■ Plate: 59
UNSTITCHED LADIES' SKIRT,
19TH CENTURY, GUJARAT.
THE SATIN GROUND
REPRESENTS ALTERNATE
ROWS OF PEACOCKS AND
FEMALE FIGURES (*PUTLIS*).

■ Plate: 61
YARDAGE, GUJARAT/VARANASI,
18TH-19TH CENTURY.
DIAGONAL BANDS FILLED IN
WITH ALTERNATING ROWS
DONE IN *GANGA JAMUNI
ZARI* AND *MINAKARI*.

and Hindu forms, seemed to act as an ilustrated pattern book for the weavers.

Floral borders, *zali* or trellises (Plate 46, page 66), and the multifarious geometrical decorations of these buildings were adopted as the chief decorative motifs by the Islamic rulers. The introduction of zoomorphic art forms[29] (Plate 112, page 131) became the new style, and animal forms were often converted into flowers and leaves. Human, animal and bird motifs were frequently incorporated into the pattern as they were the integral part of Gujarati folk tradition and this continued even after Muslim rule. Designs were noted for their rich colour schemes, red and blue being the favourites. Lions, deer or buck, parrots, and rows of elephants with riders (Plate 58, page 79) were interwoven with floral motifs like flowering shrubs or *butas*. Female figures referred to as *putlis* or dolls (Plates 59, 65; pages 80, 86) were popular motifs which probably represented an ancient folk tradition. The Gujarati cotton prints, with their beautiful designs and colours, were for centuries among India's major export items – their patterns were also adopted for the brocades.

The cosmopolitan population of the state, such as the Turks, Arabs, Mamlukes, Persians, Khurasanis and European merchants, added their influence to the existing art and craft forms. Both twill and satin weave were introduced in Gujarat. This may have been because of the large number of Persian and Central Asian weavers from Khotan, Khurasan or Balkh, who were employed in the royal workshops. These heavy silk brocades (sometimes the threads were made of three to six strands) were required for the style of dress adopted by the Muslim rulers. A variety of rich brocade furnishing fabrics were made in Ahmedabad and Surat, based on Persian prototypes. The rectangular prayer mat,[30] curtains, window covers, square fabrics used as tray covers, or put on the railings of the niches (*jharokhas*) where the emperor sat (Plates 76, 77; page 96), were popular items. The pattern format of these were based on that of Persian carpets, which had a central round medallion on which the four corner motifs were styled. The background was covered with a floral arabesque.

Gujarat brocades had a rich gold or silver metallic background on which the patterns were woven with coloured thread, giving the fabric an enamelled appearance. The technique was also known as *zarbaft*.[31] The famous Ashavali saris of Ahmedabad are of the same genre. The background of the *pallu* and border is worked in rich gold thread and woven in twill weave to reveal the maximum amount of gold thread on the surface.[32]

The double surface weave, used in the decorative end panels of the Mughal *patkas* or waistbands (Plate 66, page 87), was used by the Gujarati weavers as well. Besides being imported from Persia, they were probably made in Gujarat or in the royal workshops. These *patkas* are one of the finest examples of silk and *zari* brocades. The gold or silver grounds of the end panels of these *patkas* are beautifully decorated with floral patterns, mostly *butas*. This metallic ground has a supportive background of silk, which is visible on the reverse only. (The technique and the fabric probably can be related to the *khazz* textiles made in Khuzistan or the *khazz* weavers who came to India during the Sultanate period).

■ Plate: 62
POPAT BEL OR THE PARROT BORDER, 19TH CENTURY, GUJARAT.

Ashavali brocades, or 'the fabric of dreams or wonderland',[33] were a continuation of an old tradition kept alive on the borders and *pallus* of Ashavali saris, which were woven with mixed cotton and silk yarn.[34]

Apart from the border and *pallu* designs, *konia* (corner) motifs were used to decorate the four corners (Plate 57, page 77) - or two corners in the case of saris - of the fabric. The corner motif was usually the *carrie* (mango) shape, which is one of the most popular Indian patterns even today, used widely on every kind of textile, such as cotton prints, embroidered fabrics, Kashmiri shawls, and brocades. The origin of the pattern may have been a swaying cyprus tree, a closed bud, or a mango. It was widely adopted by Persian, Central Asian and Kashmiri shawl and carpet-weavers, particularly during the late eighteenth and nineteenth centuries, and later became popular in Europe as the 'paisley' design.

The *carrie* design of Persia and Central Asia, and the paisley of Scotland, are rather elongated and resemble a swaying cyprus tree. The Indian *carrie* is roundish and resembles a mango. The round part is called the belly (*pet* in Hindi) by the weavers and is filled with a floral or almond-shaped pattern called a *guddi*.

The *carrie* became the standard corner motif of Gujarati and Banarasi brocade saris and *dupattas*. When the upper tip was further decorated with floral creepers it was called *kalga buti* in Varanasi, because the shape resembled a turban ornament called *kalga*. Sometimes three *carries* were combined by the weavers to make an elaborate pattern that is called the 'dancing paisley'.[35]

Traditionally, the background of Ashavali saris and *dupattas* were either plain or had fine gold stripes, tiny checks or small *butis*. Later, to make them richer and heavier, trellis or *zali* of various kinds were added. The *zali* patterns were used mostly in dress material (Plate 46, page 66) or furnishing fabrics – they were named for their shapes,

■ Plate: 63
FLORAL BORDER, GUJARAT, 19TH CENTURY.

84

■ Plate: 64
FAN PIECE, LOOM FINISHED,
GUJARAT, 18TH CENTURY.
GUJARAT WAS KNOWN FOR
SUCH SPLENDID FURNISHING
FABRICS.

85

■ Plate: 65
PATKA, GUJARAT, LATE 18TH CENTURY. IT HAS A ROW OF NINE *BUTAS* OF FLOWERING HIBISCUS SHRUBS. ABOVE THESE IS THE PANEL HAVING NINE STRUTTING PEACOCKS AND NINE FEMALE FIGURES (CALLED *PUTLI* OR DOLL PATTERN).

■ Plate: 66
PATKA, GUJARAT, LATE
17TH-18TH CENTURY. FINE
CRAFTSMANSHIP, THE DESIGN
IS CREATED BY JUST USING
SHADES OF GREEN WITH
GOLD AND SILVER *ZARI*. THE
REALISTIC DEPICTION OF THE
LEAVES AND FLOWERS GIVES
IT A PAINTING-LIKE FINISH.

■ Plate: 67
GOMUKHI, GUJARAT, 19TH CENTURY. THE VALLABHA SECT USED SUCH HAND COVERS WHILE TURNING THE ROSARY.

particularly in Gujarat. A religious sect started by Vallabhacharya in the sixteenth century, called Pushti Marg, had many adherents among the affluent merchant community. Brocade accessories were made for their household temples and also for the larger community temples of Srinath Ji (Krishna), the presiding deity. Small *pichwais* (backdrops) with depictions of Lord Krishna playing the flute, surrounded by cows, are examples of the exquisite textile craftsmanship of the time. *Torans* (door hangings), *sidis* (decorative covers for the steps leading to the throne of the deity), and *gaumukhis* (gloves resembling the shape of a cow's head, used to cover rosaries held in the hand) were woven specially for the followers of the Pushti Marg.

such as *satheeya phool* (swastika and flowers), *hathi zal* (elephant), *mor zal* (peacock), *popat zal* (parrot), *dhanush zal* (bow), *badrum* (ogival), and so forth.

Religion played a significant role in the development of patterns and textiles,

References

1. Such patterns called *kech bachha* were also found on the ends of *rihas* (ladies' upper garments worn in medieval Assam) and were similar to the 'atlas' design of Uzbekistan textiles.
2. The pattern was known as *asharfi buti* (gold coin) in Banaras brocades of the nineteenth to twentieth centuries.
3. Such decorations were found on the Hoyesaleshwar Temple (ninth to tenth centuries A.D.) and in medieval textiles.
4. The technique was called *urtu* in Varanasi, and perhaps originated in the Urartu region (lying between the southern portion of the Black Sea and the Caspian Sea). It may have also had its beginnings in a civilisation which was a contemporary of the Mesopotamian civilisation.
5. Nicolo Conti, an Italian who visited Vijaynagar in 1420-21 wrote that beautiful textiles interwoven with gold were attached to the upper parts of beams in buildings to celebrate a festival (may have been flags). An envoy from the Persian king, Shahrukh, called Abdur Rajaq, presented Persian damask and satin fabric to the king. He mentions that Deva Raya II was dressed in a robe of *Zaitun* (satin).
6. Famines in Gujarat occurred in 1596, 1631, 1681, 1684, 1697, 1719, 1732 and 1747.
7. Agrawal, V.S., *Indian Art*, p. 46.
8. A rough brown bead, the round seed of a tree (mostly worn by Shaivites), to which is attributed spiritual and medicinal properties.
9. The Medieval Compositions on Indian Textiles, Chandramani Singh, Pathway to Literature, Art and Archaeology, Vol. 1, p: 176, 184.
10. These temple weavers were the *kaikkala* weavers of the Chidambaram temple. The *devangas* (also mentioned in ancient

■ Plate: 68
PICHWAI, GUJARAT, 19TH
CENURY. A SMALL *PICHWAI*
PROBABLY USED IN THE
HOUSE TEMPLES OF VALLABHA
DEVOTEES. THE PIECE IS
OUTSTANDING FOR ITS
DETAIL, COLOUR AND
RHYTHMIC FLUIDITY.

literature) were probably the weavers of the celebrated *deva* fabrics, who wove material for the deities, and were perhaps the best among all the weavers. Parvati or Chandesvari was the patron deity of the *devangas*.

11. *The Periplus of the Erythraean Sea,* written in the first century A.D., gives an account of the commerce carried on from the Red Sea and the coast of Africa to the East Indies and describes it as an important trade centre.

12. Glazier, R., *Historic Textile Fabrics*, p. 23.

13. The Madanpura (Varanasi) firm of Hazi Munna Hazi Noor, established in the mid-nineteenth century, claims that this pattern was made mainly by their family.

14. Al Beruni (A.D. 1030) mentions it in his memoirs.

15. Exquisite nine-yard saris were made for the royal houses of Baroda and the Deccan states.

16. The illustrated biography of the Mughal Emperor Shahjahan (A.D. 1628-1658) in the Windsor Castle Collection, UK.

17. *The Museum of Fine Arts Bulletin*, No. XXV, pp. 36-7, No. 149, June 1927.

18. These pieces bear a strong resemblance to a fabric seen in a sixteenth-century Mewar (Rajasthani) painting (N.C. Mehta Collection, Mumbai), depicting the story of Villhana and Champavati, where Champavati is weaving a red *lehenga* (long skirt) decorated with squares with flowers inside.

19. The same difference in weave is found in the Tanda and Dacca cotton *jamdanis*.

20. Conquered by Akbar, the Mughal Emperor, in A.D. 1600.

21. One example of this is Masulipattam, which was famed as the main centre of cotton *kalamkaris*, although they were actually made in nearby villages. Masulipattam was the trading port of the area. *Kalamkaris* were painted and printed cotton furnishing fabrics, which also became popular in Europe. Another example is Damascus in Syria, which in ancient times was the entry point for trade (between Asia and Europe).

Textiles and metalware came to be known as products of Damascus, though actually they had been made in other places.

22. The capital of the Bahamani Dynasty was founded in 1494 by Ahmed Nizam Shah, an officer in the Bahamani state. Built on the site of an ancient town called Bingar, it is said that weaving was introduced to the city by a member of the Bhagria family who was a man of considerable means and a weaver by caste.

23. Now in Maharashtra.

24. One of its rulers, Karanshah, is mentioned in the *Ain-i-Akbari* of Abul Fazl.

25. Sir George Birdwood, in his catalogue of Indian textiles, mentions a Nagpur sari made of 'silk cloth of a brilliant crimson colour, deeply bordered with gold'.

26. Ed. Majumdar, R.C., *The Struggle for Empire*, Vol. V, p. 518.

27. Ibid.

28. Gulbai Tekra in Ahmedabad was a well-known brocade-weaving area, and about three hundred families of weavers engaged in their trade there. According to the local people, weaving came to an end in this region in the beginning of the 20th century and the weavers adopted other occupations. Gulbai Tekra is now a residential area.

29. Such patterns were introduced in nineteenth-century Banaras brocades – a specimen in Bharat Kala Bhavan shows the peacock form transforming into a flower.

30. Called *ja namaz – ja* means place in Persian; *namaz* means prayer.

31. *Zar baft* in Persian; *Zar* (gold), *baftan* (woven) or woven in gold.

32. The local weaving technique was called *deshi vanat*, meaning twill weaving.

33. The Persian word *kamkhwab* or *kinkhwab*, used for such fabrics, has a similar meaning.

34. Silk was not produced in Gujarat and was imported through Khambhat from Persia, or from Assam and Bengal.

35. This was a later development. The name was given by Shri Awwal of Reori Talab, Varanasi.

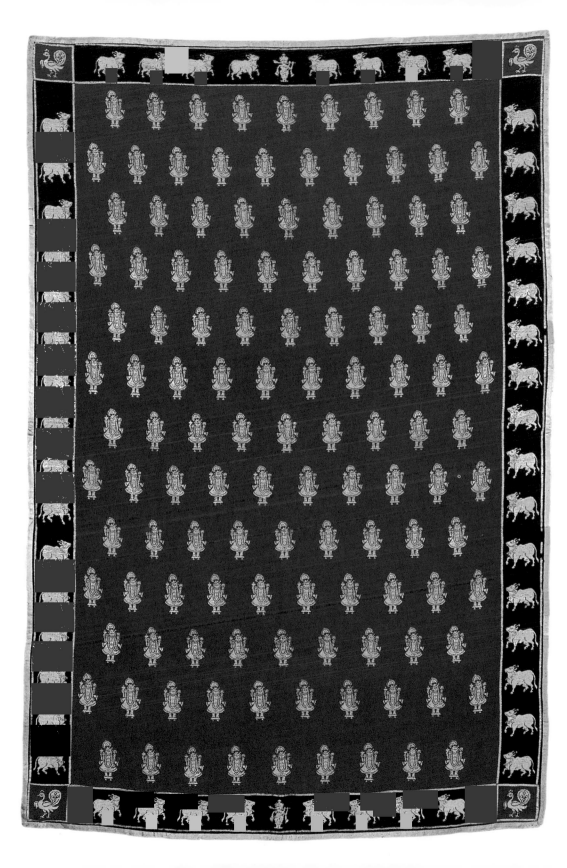

■ Plate: 69
PICHWAI, GUJARAT, 18TH
CENTURY. A NUMBER OF
SUCH BEAUTIFUL LOOM-
FINISHED FABRICS WERE
MADE FOR THE VALLABH
TEMPLE DEVOTED TO
VAISHNAVISM.

BROCADES OF NORTH INDIA

The growth of brocade-weaving centres in north India proceeded in a manner similar to those in south India. They flourished in and around royal capitals and religious or trade centres. Delhi, Lahore, Agra, Fatehpur Sikri, Varanasi, Mau, Azamgarh and Murshidabad were the main northern centres for brocade weaving. Northern weavers were greatly influenced, as far as design and technique was concerned, by the brocade-weaving regions of eastern and southern Persia, Turkey, Central Asia and Afghanistan (such as Tabrez, Isfahan, Tash Kashgar, Kamboja, Darel, Balkh, and Khotan). Royal workshops were established by the Sultanate kings of India (A.D. 1290-1526), who had come from Central Asia. They brought with them their sartorial tradition and employed weavers to suit their requirements. Expert weavers from those distant lands worked with the local weavers and imparted their skills to them. Brocades produced at the royal workshops of other well-known Muslim centres in Syria, Egypt, Turkey and Persia were also exported to India.

Though regrettably we lack textile samples from the Sultanate period, architectural decorations of the period give us an idea of the decorative motifs used. Arabesque, trellises, floral scrolls and calligraphic decorations were the salient features of the Sultanate motifs.

The stucco decorations carved on the walls of an ancient mosque in Balkh[1] (A.D. 848, Afghanistan; Plate 71) give us a good idea about popular medieval motifs. Grape vines, palmettes, cones, pomegranates, circles and other interlocking geometrical patterns, such as squares and circles enclosing floral patterns, are seen later too. *Carries*, represented on these wall decorations, are probably one of the earliest representations of this celebrated motif of later years. Similarly, the zigzag borders, floral swirls (Plate 72) and floral *zal* patterns used in later Banaras brocades can be traced to the designs in this mosque. Balkh itself was a known weaving centre since the ancient period. It seems like the southern and western Indian weavers and the central Asian weavers too shared the decorative motifs with the architectural decorations of this region.

MUGHAL BROCADES (A.D. 1526 TO 1857)

The Mughal Empire was founded in India in A.D. 1526 by Babar, a chieftain of Fargana in Samarkand. This was a period of a great revival of Indian art and crafts. Other

■ Plate: 71
ANCIENT ABBASID MOSQUE
AT BALKH (AFGHANISTAN).
A.D. 848, KNOWN AS MASJID-
I-TARIKH. THE CONTINUITY
OF THE VARIOUS
ARCHITECTURAL DECORATIVE
MOTIFS SEEN ON THIS
MOSQUE CAN BE TRACED AS
A TEXTILE PATTERN EVEN A
THOUSAND YEARS LATER
AND IN ENTIRELY DIFFERENT
REGIONS. HERE THE STAR-
SHAPED GEOMETRICAL
PATTERN ENCLOSING A
SWIRLING FLOWER-LIKE
MOTIF SEEN ON THE MOSQUE
PILLAR CAN BE COMPARED
WITH THE 19TH-CENTURY
BANARAS BROCADE (PLATE
72). LOCALLY, IT IS CALLED
THE *CHARKHI* OR *JALEBI BUTI.*

Preceding page 92

■ Plate: 70
YARDAGE, GUJARAT/VARANASI,
LATE 18TH CENTURY. THIS
MOTIF, THE *PANKHA BUTA*, IS
INFLUENCED BY THE TURKISH
BROCADE OF THE 17TH
CENTURY.

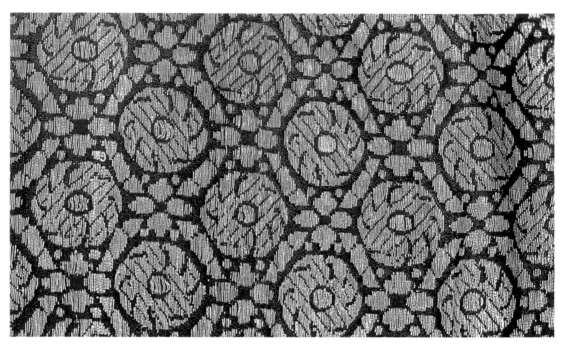

illustrious emperors of this dynasty – Humayun, Akbar, Jahangir, Shahjahan and Aurangzeb – favoured a highly sophisticated culture, which was the synthesis of central Asian, Persian, and Indian traditions. Initiated by Akbar, Mughal art reached its zenith during the period of Jahangir and Shahjahan (A.D. 1606-1648), and vied with Persian art. The royal workshops of the Mughals at Ahmedabad, Delhi, Lahore, Fatehpur Sikri and Agra produced beautiful and expensive brocades (which were used to make garments and furnishings and were presented as gifts to meritorious courtiers or foreign envoys). Both Indian and foreign weavers worked in these workshops under the eagle eye of the emperor's supervisors. The emperors also took an interest in the design and production of the various fabrics.

Abul Fazl mentions in *Ain-i-Akbari* that 'skilful makers and workmen have settled in this country to teach an imported system of manufacturing.' He gives a list of expensive brocade textiles that were imported from Persia, Turkey, Iraq, Central Asia and Europe.

Gujarati masons and weavers were brought by Akbar to the royal workshops after his conquest of the province in A.D. 1572. According to Abul Fazl, Akbar took an active role in overseeing the royal textile workshops established at Lahore, Agra and Fatehpur Sikri, where skilled weavers from different regions worked.

Some brocades mentioned in Sultanate literature continued to be popular in the Mughal period too. Two seventeenth century Rajasthani works, *Kapada Chintani* and *Kapada Kutuhal* (mentioned earlier) give an account of the costumes and textiles of the period, described as costly and beautiful fabrics. A few examples are: *Misanjar (Mushazzar), Kamkhani (Kamkha), Jarkas (Zarkashi,* that can be gold embroidered), *Illaycha (Alcha), Chira, Pat,* and *Dudami.*

Mughal brocades had a sophistication and beauty of their own. The use of gold and silver threads and a variety of multicoloured motifs imparted to them magnificence and splendour, elevating the craft of the weaver to that of a superior art. For designs and colour schemes they could count on the liberal assistance of artists, draftsmen and painters employed in the royal atelier. Patterns were mainly inspired by the decorative paintings of the Mughal court painters, particularly the floral or geometric

patterns made on the decorative borders (*hashiya*) of these paintings.

Weavers from different countries and cultures, working under one roof, were able to imbibe some of the best aspects of each others' traditions. This intermingling of creative techniques brought about a great transformation in the textile-weaving industry – the exquisite *latifa* (beautiful) *buti* (Plate 84, page 98) was the outcome of a fusion of Persian and Indian designs. The Gujarati weavers, for instance, brought with them their repertoire of indigenous designs, such as floral scrolls, lush vegetal embellishments, and animal and bird motifs.

Persian brocades (Plates 73, 74) had a predominant influence on Mughal brocades. This was facilitated by the positive political relationship of the Mughals with

Left to right

■ Plate: 73
SILK FRAGMENT, PERSIA, 17TH CENTURY, BROCADE. IRIS PLANT ON A SILVER GROUND IN SILK.

■ Plate: 74
SILK FRAGMENT, PERSIA, 18TH CENTURY, BROCADE. SMALL CARNATIONS IN HORIZONTAL REGISTER WOVEN WITH GOLD THREAD ON PERSIAN BLUE GROUND.

■ Plate: 75
SILK FRAGMENT, GUJARAT, 18TH CENTURY. FINE EXAMPLE OF *GANGA JAMUNI* AND *MINAKARI* WORK.

■ Plate: 76
SHAHJAHAN SITTING IN
JHAROKHA. A *DARBAR* PAINTING
FROM THE *BADSHAHNAMAH*
PAINTED A.D. 1650. THE
EMPEROR AND OTHER
COURTIERS ARE SHOWN
WEARING *JAMAS* WITH
SINGLE FLOWER MOTIFS.

Right

■ Plate: 77
ASAN, GUJARAT, 17TH
CENTURY. SUCH SMALL,
USUALLY SQUARE OR OBLONG
DECORATIVE CARPETS WERE
USED AS PARAPET COVERS IN
ROYAL APARTMENTS AND
COURTS.

Persia from the time of Humayun, who spent his years of exile in the court of Shah Tahmasp of Persia (A.D. 1524-1576). This was the golden age of Persian art and craft, and most Muslim courts in western and central Asia emulated them. Later, Humayun re-established his empire in India and brought with him two Persian masters, Mir Sayyad Ali and Abdus Samad, who formed the nucleus of the Mughal painting tradition.[2]

The exchange of high-ranking envoys between the two countries became a regular practice (which continued throughout the Mughal period), and the choicest gifts were exchanged and the exquisite brocades of Persia were one of the most favoured presents.

Also, the Persian brocades were copied in the Mughal workshops. Sometimes they are so nearly identical that it is almost impossible to distinguish between them (Plates 16, 17; page 35). Examples of this can be seen at the Bharat Kala Bhavan in Varanasi and at the AEDTA (Association pour l'Etude et la Documentation des Textiles des Asie) collection of *patkas*, furnishing and dress material (Plates 14, 16, 17, 18, 21; pages 32, 35, 36, 37).

As compared to Persian prototypes, the designs executed in Mughal courts were more realistic and less decorative. The difference between Mughal and Persian art is well defined by Dr A.N. Ganguly.[3] He writes, 'the Persian manner from beginning to end is almost an art of book illustration, a decorative embellishment to a fine book, and is characterised by an intense feeling for decoration, satisfied by curious, conventional devices and ornamental

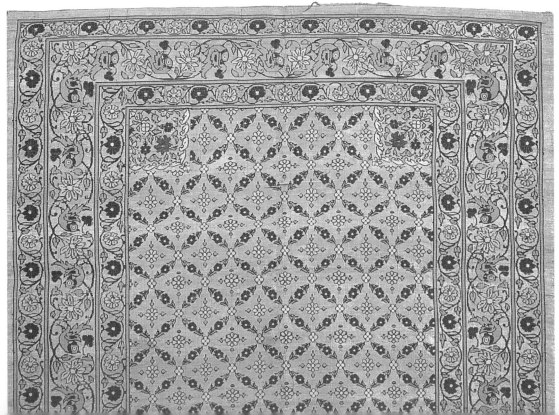

schemes, not only in the rendering of landscape and trees, but also in the schematic and conventional rendering of human faces and gestures. The Persian leaves of trees receive a flat ornamental treatment and the plants are depicted in schematic form. The Mughal school, though it borrows many elements of decoration, is essentially an art of a realistic preservation of actual scenes and characters.'

Instructions laid down in the *Hadis*[4] prohibited the depiction of living creatures in any form of Islamic art. Thus, animals, birds, human figures, so frequently used in pre-Muslim Persian and Sassanid textiles, were mostly replaced by floral and geometrical forms. But a revival took place in Persia in A.D. 1499 under the Safiddian dynasty (when the rulers were the natives of Persia for the first time since the days of the Sassanian kings). Art and culture were redefined in a new way, which clearly set them apart from the art of other contemporary Muslim dynasties. The art of the Safiddian period reached its zenith under Shah Abbas (A.D. 1586-1625). It was a period of remarkable achievement in the production of splendid carpets, silk brocades and velvets, with their distinctive technique, design and colour. The rulers kept art free from religion, and Persian weavers celebrated this freedom, reviving many Sassanian motifs, such as hunting scenes[5] and figural motifs. Animal motifs were depicted in both realistic and stylised forms. The imagery used in Persian prose and poetry, such as heavenly gardens with fairies and human figures, trees, birds, and so forth, were woven into textiles as well.

The perfect integration of such patterns into the decorative background was typical of Persian craftsmanship.

Such figured textiles of exceptional beauty, made in Persian workshops, became popular in the Mughal court. Jahangir, a contemporary of Shah Abbas, who was known for his love of the rare and unusual, imported such fabrics from Persia or had them made in his royal workshops.

As is seen in a rare *patka* of the Jahangir period in the Bharat Kala Bhavan collection (Plate 81, page 100), the decorative theme on its long end panels is probably the depiction of the joys of paradise or the Garden of Delight, a popular Persian motif of the fifteenth and sixteenth centuries. Three long vine creepers intermingle with a variety of birds, flying or sitting, among them parrots, simurg (a mythical Persian bird), and peacocks. Two human figures are shown sitting amidst the creeper, drinking from their vessels. One of them, well-dressed with his lower body turning like a ploughshare, could be a male angel.[6] This piece, probably a copy of a Persian prototype, was woven at a Gujarati centre. The human faces in profile with long eyes betray the western Indian manuscript painting tradition of the sixteenth century.

The depiction of animals, birds and human figures can also be seen on painted panels on the tomb of Itmad-ud-daulah in Agra, built between A.D. 1622-1627 for the parents of Nurjahan, Jahangir's beloved wife. Cups and wine glasses, so characteristic of Jahangir's reign, are depicted in the inlaid marble, and human figures in sitting postures merge with the floral pattern, as

■ Plate: 84
LATIFA BUTA, 19TH CENTURY,
VARANASI. CLOSELY
ARRANGED ROWS OF *GANGA
JAMUNI ZARI*-WORKED
FLOWERING PLANT IN
ALMOND FORMAT.

98

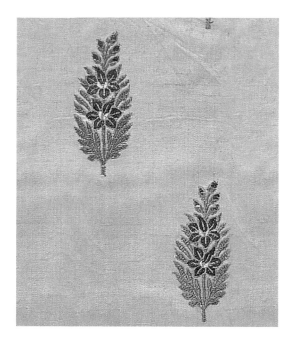

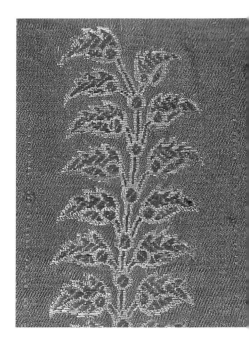

seen in the *patku* pattern in the Bharat Kala Bhavan collection, which makes it a typical example of the silk brocade produced during Jahangir's reign.

An embroidered riding jacket of Jahangir's period, in the Victoria and Albert Museum, London, is another example of the figural pattern. It is decorated with the 'repeating pattern of animals, birds and winged insects in a rocky landscape of trees and flowers, with great cats seen devouring their prey or reposing peacefully in the shade'.[7] Based on a Persian motif, it is also seen in the textile and decorative art of the eighteenth and nineteenth centuries[8] and popularly known as the *shikargah* pattern (Plates 85, 95; pages 102, 110). The design was popularised by the provincial Mughal courts, particularly those in the Deccan, Gujarat, Awadh and Murshidabad.

Apart from Persian influence, such figural patterned brocades were popular during Jahangir's reign because of his predilection for figural motifs, inspired by European pictoral engravings and tapestries. His daring and inquisitive nature attracted him to rarities and novelties.[10]

Another motif of Persian origin, which became popular in eighteenth and nineteenth-century Kashmiri shawls and Gujarat and Banaras brocades, were rows of floral *butis* with birds in between.[16]

Early Mughal patterns were bold, realistic, simple, and there was ample space between the floral motifs. Designs stood out prominently against the background (Plates 83, 91; pages 101, 106). Complex patterns were developed only when additional decorative elements were included in the basic pattern. During later periods, the gap

Left to right

■ Plate: 78
BROCADE FRAGMENT, 17TH CENTURY, MUGHAL. FLORAL *BUTI* ON A CREAMISH SILK GROUND; A GOLD *ZARI* OUTLINE THAT EXTENDS TO FLOWERS' VEINS MAKES THE MOTIF DELICATE. SUCH *BUTIS* WERE IN FASHION DURING SHAHJAHAN'S TIME.

■ Plate: 79
SILK FRAGMENT (*HIMRU*), 17TH CENTURY, MUGHAL. THE POPPY PLANT IS SIMILAR TO PERSIAN EXAMPLES.

■ Plate: 80
SILK FRAGMENT, 17TH CENTURY, WESTERN INDIA. THE SPRIG PATTERN WITH DECORATIVE LEAVES IS OUTLINED WITH GOLD *ZARI*.

■ Plate: 81
MUGHAL *PATKA*, EARLY 17TH
CENTURY. MUGHAL *PATKAS*
ARE THE BEST EXAMPLES OF
CULTURAL INFLUENCES ON
TECHNIQUE AND DESIGN
MAYBE BECAUSE THE *PATKA*
WAS A PART OF THE COURT
DRESS OF PERSIA, TURKEY,
CENTRAL ASIA, OR INDIA.

Top

■ Plate: 82
PATKA, EARLY 17TH CENTURY.
FLOWERING PLANTS RESEMBLE
THE STYLISED CHINESE
CLOUD FORM.

Right

■ Plate: 83
LOOM-FINISHED CURTAIN,
LAMPAS, MUGHAL, 17TH
CENTURY, AGRA/LAHORE.
SUCH TEXTILES ARE PROBABLY
THE PRODUCT OF ROYAL
WORKSHOPS.

101

■ Plate: 85
SILK FRAGMENT, 19TH
CENTURY, VARANASI. A
HUNTING SCENE DEPICTS
TIGERS AND DEERS.
RECLINING DEERS WERE
USED FREQUENTLY IN THE
10TH-13TH CENTURY
CHINESE BROCADES.

Facing page

■ Plate: 86
DUPATTA, VARANASI, EARKY
20TH CENTURY. THE *PALLU*
PATTERN AT BOTH ENDS
CONSISTS OF ROWS OF
TWELVE *BUTAS* OF
CHRYSANTHEMUMS
IN GOLD *ZARI.*

between the motifs was also filled with smaller motifs or geometrical forms.

The flowering plant emerged as the dominant motif in Mughal art and craft, 'not only in album borders but also as an architectural decoration (as in the carved stone and *pietra dura* work in such buildings as the Taj Mahal in Agra and the Red Fort in Delhi), as well as in sashes, robes, metal work, jade carving, and in fact in almost every aspect of artistic endeavour.'[11]

Jahangir's visit to Kashmir in the spring of A.D. 1620 had much to do with these exquisite representations of floral and animal motifs being introduced in Mughal art. The other influence, as suggested by some noted scholars such as Robert Skelton, was that of engraved European herbal books. The Jesuits brought with them devotional, religious or classical prints with decorative borders which contained numerous illustrations with flowering plants in the borders, some even with butterflies and insects! It is interesting to note that the iris and narcissus flowers, which became celebrated Mughal motifs, appear frequently in these borders with tulips, poppies, primulas, roses and lilies. The Emperor ordered the court painter Mansur to copy flowers growing in the Kashmir valley in the style of these herbal illustrations, which became the principal motifs of Mughal decorative art.

The motifs which were popular during Shahjahan's reign (A.D. 1628-1648) display a classical harmony of proportion (Plate 83). Floral motifs were used abundantly, though compared to the realistic forms of Jahangir's time, they were rather formal. In the words of Stuart Cary Welch, they used 'a hypnotic arrangement of blossoms, which strikes a perfect balance between naturalism and abstraction.'[12] This is evident in the beautiful court-scene paintings of Shahjahan's period – the rigid rows of courtiers standing in a strictly disciplined manner imparts a formal tone to the magnificent paintings. The religious orthodoxy of Shahjahan made him disapprove of figural patterns on Indian, European or Safavid brocades, so popular during Jahangir's reign. He disapproved of his father's preferences, which for him were 'old fashioned and in bad taste', though such brocades (used mainly as furnishing fabrics), depicting scenes of paradise with fairies and idealised garden motifs (Plate 81), can be seen in the paintings of the *Badshahnamah,* the history of his reign. One such painting shows Shahjahan and his son, Prince Dara Shikoh, sitting together, leaning against a bolster covered with a brilliantly coloured, rich *safavid* figural brocade. In another painting, Jahangir is shown resting against a bolster covered with a similarly patterned fabric. The same type of fabric was used as upholstery, elephant trappings, saddle-cloths, tray covers, and so forth. Some courtiers of Jahangir's period are also shown wearing such figural brocades. One of them, Riza Bahadur (known as *khidmadgar* Khan or chief servant), is shown wearing a double-breasted *jama* (long upper garment) made of a similarly patterned brocade in a court scene[13] – his tricoloured headdress (*sahrang pagri*) is tied differently too. Inayat Khan, a favourite courtier in Jahangir's court, is shown wearing a pyjama of this figural brocade. Seeing these textiles in the paintings of the *Badshahnamah* does not, however, mean that this was a popular pattern during Shahjahan's reign. In fact, such fabrics were usually used as furnishing material which were kept in the royal *toshakkhana*,[14] and continued to be used for generations. The courtiers' garments had most likely been presented to them by Jahangir, to be worn on special occasions.[15]

The gorgeous gold and silver brocades with their enamel-like decorations can be seen in a number of paintings from Shahjahan's period, known for their minute details. Paintings from the *Badshahnamah* display the splendour of Mughal textiles, both in costumes and as furnishing material, that were used as palace and court decorations. The main patterns were floral

arabesques, geometrical trellis designs, and the ogival, surrounded by decorative borders. The chronicle mentions that among the other wedding gifts to Prince Dara Shikoh were 'various sorts of brocades from Hindustan, Persia, Anatolia, China and Europe, various carpets, rugs, canopies in goldspun and gold embroidered velvet, and other things from the workshops, suitable for mighty emperors.'

The courtiers are shown wearing two types of *patkas* – one has a plain white ground (probably of cotton or silk gauze), with richly patterned borders of the type made at Paithan, Chanderi and Burhanpur (mentioned earlier) and the other has a horizontal, striped, coloured silk ground,

with richly decorated ends. They are referred to as Mughal *patkas*. Some of the patterns betray their foreign origin – one such example being the Chinese cloud pattern, popular in sixteenth-century Turkish brocades (Plate 82, page 101). These probably are the best examples of intercultural influences on technique and designs shared by Indian, Persian, Turkish and central Asian brocade pieces which makes it difficult to tell the place of their origin, particularly in Indian and Persian examples. The other centres can be Samarkand and Bukhara. In India they were probably the product of royal workshops or were made at centres like Burhanpur (Deccan), Ahmedabad or Surat. The characteristic of this group of *patkas* is

104

the 'double layer' weaving technique used for decorating rich end panels. Against the gold or silver ground the patterns, usually the flowering plants, are woven using minimum colours and bring out some of the finest example of silk brocades. Mostly the examples have survived in fragments or in a torn condition. The reason is they were heavily starched, therefore, when folded they tend to crack at the folds.

Some of the panel patterns of these *patkas* were seen on the later Ashavali saris of Gujarat. A similarity can be traced also between the ground pattern of these *patkas*, particularly the horizontal decorative stripes and trellis with yardage fabrics of some southern an western Indian centres. This corroborates the theory in India that they were made most probably in Ahmedabad or Burhanpur.

The perfection of pattern achieved during the reign of Shahjahan can be credited to the fact that the Emperor met his artists frequently to supervise their work. Elegance and symmetry in the arrangement of motifs are the hallmarks of the patterns of his period. Different floral forms,[16] such as roses, poppies, tulips, marigolds, narcissi, peonies, jasmine, and *champa* were used in a highly disciplined and orderly manner.

Though the religious orthodoxy of Shahjahan and Aurangzeb condemned any figural designs and reverted to the floral decoration sanctioned by Islam, Shahjahan

Following pages 106-107

■ Plate: 91
PATKA, MID-17TH CENTURY. A TYPICAL *SHAHJAHANI BUTA* WITH RIBBON-LIKE LEAVES, DROOPING *SOSAN* FLOWER, AND BUDS ON A GOLD *ZARI* GROUND.

■ Plate: 92
PATKA FRAGMENT, 17TH CENTURY. HIBISCUS PLANTS WITH FLOWERS SHOWN ON THE SILVER GROUND.

may have taken advantage of the fact that Suleman was the Quranic patron saint of birds and animals, and used this as an excuse to depict animals and birds in the art of his period. The peacock became the primary bird motif during his reign, and the lion, bull, sheep, bird and butterfly designs were incorporated into the floral patterns.

Shahjahan's love of architecture, gardens and flowers had a great impact on the decorative art of his period – a pattern called *charbagh* (the literal meaning is the four gardens) was probably inspired by the Shalimar Bagh.[17] Mughal gardens were usually divided into four parts, with a fountain in the centre. Similarly, shawls and *odhnis* were divided into squares of four different colours with a central medallion and four corner patterns (Plate 93). This design was used in nineteenth-century Kashmir shawls, canopies and Banarasi *chaukora* (square) veils too. In Varanasi, this weaving technique is called *rangkat,*[18] in which one colour is used for the warp and four different coloured threads for the weft, to form the four colour squares.

The designs of Aurangzeb's period were repetitions of the motifs used during Shahjahan's reign. They, however, lost their previous naturalism in favour of ostentation. As observed by Welch, 'their identity has disappeared in the craftsmen's concentration upon decorative and rhythmic pattern.'[19] This was the period of a general decline in art, reflected also in the Emperor's attitude towards art and craft.

Lahore, one of the important silk brocade-weaving centres of the Mughal period, was an active textile centre even

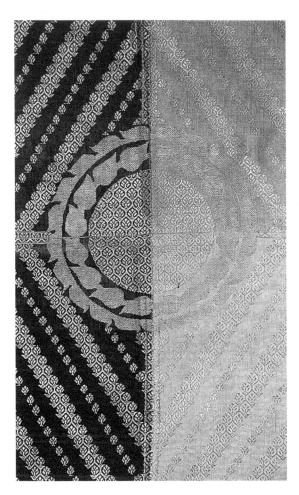

■ Plate: 93
CHAUKORA DUPATTA,
VARANASI, 19TH CENTURY.
THE *CHAUKORA* OR THE
SQUARE VEIL HAS THE
CHARBAGH PATTERN MADE
WITH THE *RANGKAT* ('BREAK
OF COLOUR') TECHNIQUE.

Facing page

■ Plate: 94
JAMA, PROBABLY LAHORE,
19TH CENTURY. A
DAMASCUSED MAROON
SATIN GROUND HAS
MEENAKARI AND GOLD *ZARI
BUTIS* AND A *SANJAB* BORDER
TUCKED ON EDGE.

employed in Lahore workshops, made brocades and satin damask similar to those of their own country. It is mentioned in the *Tuzuk-i-Jahangiri* that more than a hundred gold brocades were sent by Murtaza Khan, the Governor of Lahore, as a present for Jahangir, to celebrate the eleventh year of his rule in A.D. 1616.

Mughal emperors and courtiers are often shown wearing fine 'self-patterned', coloured *jamas* in paintings. Such fine silk textiles were made in Lahore too and continued to be made there till at least the midde of the nineteenth century. *The Royal Gazetteer* of 1885 mentions that Lahore was known for producing fine satin damask and silk brocades, and that the industry was adversely affected because the silk thread imported from Bukhara had stopped being exported.

A blend of the Hindu and Saracenic styles of decoration, adopted in the Kashi panels (glazed tile with inlay work), which covered about eight hundred square yards of the Lahore Fort, are an example of the style adopted in Lahore's decorative arts, including textiles – figural designs of humans, animals, birds and hunting scenes were used with floral motifs. The liberal religious attitude of both Akbar and Jahangir, and the revival of old Sassanid patterns in contemporary Persian art during their time, encouraged the development of such designs.

BROCADES IN THE LATER MUGHAL PERIOD

The disintegration of the Mughal Empire after the death of Aurangzeb in A.D. 1707

during the Sultanate period. It was the royal residence of the Mughals and grew to be, in the words of Abul Fazl, 'the grand resort of people of all nations.'[20] The royal workshops of Lahore were well known for their gold and silver brocades (gold and silver threads were also manufactured), and the silk weavers were renowned for their superior fabrics, made of Bukhara thread – it is probable that weavers from Bukhara,[21] Samarkand and other central Asian centres,

resulted in the autonomy of many provincial rulers, who followed the Mughal tradition and patronised many craftsmen and artists. Some of them may have come from the erstwhile royal workshops of the Mughals, particularly those working for the royal courts of Awadh and Murshidabad.

The Shia Muslim rulers of Awadh traced their origin to Persia, and their culture was highly influenced by Persian customs and style. Figural motifs, such as the hunting scene, were popular (as were floral designs), and their dress code was also influenced by Persian fashions. A portrait of Shuja-ud-Daula, the Nawab of Awadh, shows him wearing a long *badrum*-patterned brocade *jama* in the Persian style (reaching below the knees) with decorative *sanjab* borders. The *nadiri*[22] worn by him has a long fur collar, and *shikargah*-pattern with a horse and rider, elephant, and human figures intermingling with floral *buta*s.

■ Plate: 95
CHOGA (BACK), VARANASI, EARLY 20TH
CENTURY. AN OUTSTANDING PIECE
WOVEN ACCORDING TO THE CUT OF
THE GARMENT. ITS GROUND IS FILLED
WITH THE *ZARI KALGA* AND *SHIKARGARH*
PATTERN.

Facing page (clockwise, from left)

■ Plate: 96
CHILD'S COAT, VARANASI, 19TH
CENTURY. THE COAT AND OTHER
PIECES HERE SHOW THE INFLUENCE OF
THE MEANDERING PATTERN POPULAR
IN 18TH-CENTURY FRENCH BROCADES.

■ Plate: 97
SKIRT, VARANASI, 19TH CENTURY. A
GANGA-JAMUNI ZARI PATTERN OF
DIAGONAL CREEPERS AND *LAHRIYA*.

■ Plate: 98
MEN'S PYJAMA, VARANASI, 19TH
CENTURY. THE ZIGZAG PATTERN WAS
QUITE FASHIONABLE IN THE MUGHAL
AND AWADH COURTS; THE IDEA WAS
TO CREATE THE EFFECT OF RUNNING
WATER AND FLOWER BEDS.

Top

■ Plate: 99
JAMA, HIMRU, MURSHIDABAD,
19TH CENTURY.

Right

■ Plate: 100
JACKET MADE OF HIMRU
FABRIC, MURSHIDABAD,
19TH CENTURY.

Facing page

■ Plate: 101
BALUCHARI SARI,
MURSHIDABAD (BENGAL),
1860. THE HIMRU BROCADE
SARI HAS A BROAD *PALLU*
DIVIDED INTO DIFFERENTLY
PATTERNED PANELS.

Mau, Azamgarh, Jalalabad and Kanauj were the main weaving centres, but Varanasi was the main supplier of brocade fabrics in the kingdom of Awadh. In the late nineteenth century, the only class of weavers left in Lucknow were called the *daryayi baf*, who made a silk fabric called *daryayi,* which was about nine inches wide and had fine gold and silver stripes. These were usually stitched on as the borders of brocade garments or *zari dupattas*. There was a great demand for these fabrics which were used as decorative accessories. In the nineteenth-century Awadh court, richly decorated brocade garments were in fashion, and gold and silver embroidery (*zardozi*) was popular, often combined with pearls and semi-precious stones. Besides this, a number of decorative accessories, such as *gota, patha, gokhru (*gold and silver ribbons), *salma, sitara* and *daryayi* fabric were used to enrich garments. But *daryayi* was replaced by

English sarsenet,[23] a fine damask silk used mainly to line garments. Some *daryayi* weavers probably shifted to Varanasi, because till 1940-50 there were still a few weavers in the city who made *daryayi* (also called *tamami),* which was used as decorative borders.

Murshidabad, founded by Murshid Quli Khan in A.D. 1706, became a flourishing silk centre. Kasimbazar and Behrampur were the main silk-trading centres in Bengal – the English, French, Dutch and Armenians all traded in silk, which was one of the oldest industries in the province. After the battle of Plassey in A.D. 1757, the silk trade was dominated by the English. Tavernier in his travel accounts wrote that most of the raw silk produced in and around Bengal and Assam was sent to workshops in Gujarat. He says, 'All the silks are brought to the kingdom of Gujarat, and the greater part come to Ahmedabad and Surat, where they are woven into fabrics. The finest carpets of silk and gold are made in Surat.' By 'carpets' he meant the small oblong or square furnishing mats mentioned earlier.

In the eighteenth century, Bengal became the main British trading centre under the East India Company, and the trading centres of other Indian provinces, particularly Gujarat, dwindled. This must have affected the brocade industry of Gujarat and other southern centres, which were the largest users of silver thread (silver being imported by the British company) and silk. Besides natural calamities such as famine or drought, this must have been the cause of the migration of traders and weavers from Gujarat and Rajasthan to

■ Plate: 102
SILK SHAWL, HIMRU, 19TH
CENTURY, BENGAL. SUCH
SHAWLS WERE PROBABLY
MADE FOR NOBLES OR THE
ARMENIAN SILK TRADERS OF
BENGAL.

Bottom
■ Plate: 104
SILK FRAGMENT, 19TH
CENTURY, PROBABLY MADE IN
DACCA (BENGAL).

Facing page
■ Plate: 103
YARDAGE, LATE 19TH-20TH
CENTURY, *BADRUM* PATTERN,
VARANASI.

northeastern centres like Murshidabad (mainly at Azimgani and Baluchar) and Varanasi. By the end of the eighteenth century, both Murshidabad and Varanasi became great silk brocade-weaving centres. The similarity between the patterns of the borders and *butis* of Baluchari saris and designs indigenous to Gujarat substantiates this theory (Plate 102).

Balucharis, the celebrated figure-patterned saris of Bengal (Plate 101, page 113), were named after the village Baluchar in Murshidabad district. The unique pattern placement woven with different-coloured silk threads on silk fabric, without any use of *zari* became famous. The long *pallu* usually had two to four big *kalgas* (*carrie*) motifs in the centre surrounded by smaller square compartments depicting Indian and European nobles engaged in various activities such as smoking a hookah, playing chess, reading a book, riding an elephant or horse, smelling a flower, and so forth. The domination of the British East India Company, their involvement in sericulture, and the rise of local landlords (*zamindars*) patronised by the British, had a powerful effect on contemporary society, which was expressed in Baluchari patterns. The coming of the railway to India in the mid-nineteenth century was a big event and was invariably used as a motif in these saris. This indicates the artists' awareness of their surroundings, their boldness, and the freedom they enjoyed, which allowed them to introduce such unconventional patterns in textiles. Besides the decorative *pallu*, the saris had (and still have) a floral creeper border all around with small flower *butis* on the 'ground'.

The other weaving centres in Murshidabad district were Sujaganj, Daulatabazar, Bhagwangala, Goas, Manullabazar, Assanpur and Mirzapur. According to Major Walsh, Mirzapur boasted of the most skilled weavers in the district. Behrampur and Murshidabad were the main trading centres for both raw silk and finished fabrics.

The end panels of some of the lady's upper garments, called *riha,* had multicoloured bands of parallel stripes in yellow, green or white. According to Dr R. Dasgupta, 'The design known as *kesh bachha reha* is also similar to the Atlas design of Uzbekistan textiles. But while the colours of Altas run into one another, *kesh baccha* colours are strictly and sharply demarcated as in the Uzbek *bekasam* design.'[24] These Central Asian patterns were popular probably due to the involvement of Armenians in the silk trade.

Jhardar probably referred to fabric or saris with a floral pattern or creeper design. *Mosaris* or *masaharis* (mosquito nets) were made too. They were also used as dress material or to line the garments.

Mutka or *matka* silk woven in Murshidabad was mainly used by the Hindus during the rituals or while cooking or eating food. Suit lengths and large pocket handkerchiefs of *matka* silk were popular

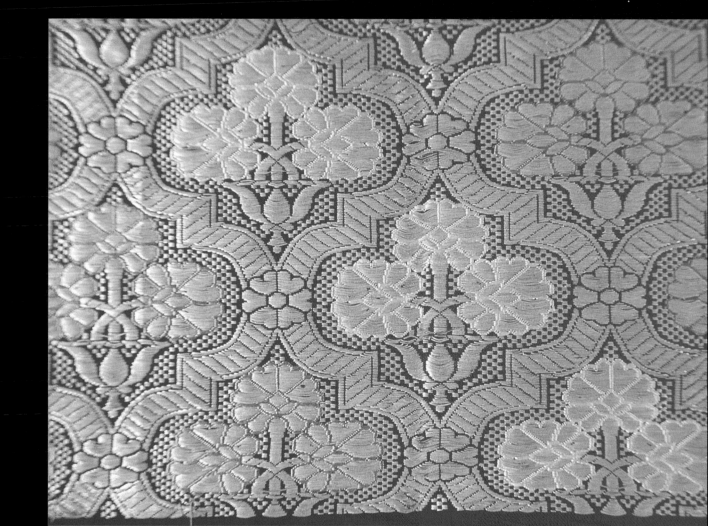

among the English.[25] The material was used locally and in other parts of India. Till the late nineteenth century, it was also exported to countries like Arabia and Persia, via Bombay.

Bengal silk was usually yellow, but white was also available. Vegetable dyes were used to obtain deep blue, red, pink, yellow, orange, purple and chocolate colours. Though green was used too, it was not permanant – the art of producing a colour-fast green was unknown to the Murshidabad dyers. Aniline dyes, introduced from Europe around the late nineteenth century, were easier to use and more brilliant in colour, but compared to the indigenous dyes they were less permanent.

WESTERN INFLUENCE ON LATER MUGHAL BROCADES

Diminishing Mughal power after the death of Aurangzeb in A.D. 1707 brought many political and cultural changes. Provincial rulers became independent and powerful. Also India was exposed to western power, particularly the English and the French. From the eighteenth century, changes were evident both in dress fashions and textile designs, which were often made keeping in view the western market. Illustrated books with western patterns were introduced to Indian textile manufactures, who copied them.

The phenomenal success of the French brocade industry in Lyons brought French brocades into high fashion. Jean Revel (A.D. 1684-1751), a well-known designer from Lyons, specialised in designing fantastic flower patterns and chinoiserie.[26] Revel also introduced a weaving technique called *point rentre*, which gave the effect of light and shade. It was introduced in Varanasi in Badi Bazar in the late nineteenth or early twentieth century. Another French pattern, invented by Lyons designers, which greatly influenced Indian brocade weavers of the late eighteenth or nineteenth century, was the meandering pattern (Plates 96, 97, 98; page 111), popular in France between A.D. 1750-1770. Influenced by the Pompadour[27] style of the period, decorative motifs like ribbons, bands of lace, frills, bows, spotted fur or floral sprays were incorporated into the meandering pattern, which was woven in a flowing undulating design (vertically or diagonally) on the textile. This pattern was considered the acme of grace and beauty in eighteenth-century French and English society. Italian (Venice), English (Spitalfields) and French (Lyons) brocade weavers were influenced by each other's designs. They responded to the demands of the royalty and the aristocracy. These fabrics became very popular in aristocratic Indian society too, and their designs greatly affected Indian brocades. The introduction of the jacquard loom[28] in France in A.D. 1804 revolutionised the weaving industry. In India, it was first introduced in Gujarat in the late nineteenth century and increased the speed of weavers significantly.

Towards the end of the eighteenth century, patterned silks produced in English factories in Spitalfields[29] and Norwich were exported to the Indian markets. These European patterns and colours (Plate 105) were copied both for export and the home market. The growing influence of British culture on Indian society influenced the sartorial taste too, particularly in the case of men. Simpler designs, dotted patterns or small sprigs of flowers, were preferred. Often plain or self-patterned fabrics were simply decorated with embroidered or brocade borders only at the pocket, collar and sleeves.

To capture the market monopolised by Indian fabrics (primarily cotton), the British government banned the import of textiles from India and Persia, which badly affected the Indian cotton industry, but only partially affected the brocade industry. First, the brocades, renowned for their beauty of detail, harmonious lines and perfection of ornamentation, and their intricate handwoven patterns often using five to six colours in a single design could not be reproduced on jacquard looms. Second, the cost of British imports in India was excessive. The ban was lifted in the nineteenth century, but some British influence remained, both on Indian designs and technique.

European influence came indirectly to India through Persian brocades, which were also highly influenced by contemporary European patterns and used decorative themes taken from European engravings and printed books popular at that time. Though there was a marked decline in the Persian silk trade in the eighteenth century, Persia still exported patterned brocades, damask, satin and *chaharzari* (a particular length of fabric) to India and other neighbouring countries like Turkey, Russia, Bukhara and Afganistan. This may have

Facing page

■ Plate: 105
SARI, VARANASI, 1940. WITH APPARENT WESTERN INFLUENCE THE PATTERN WAS WOVEN ON FINE *KATAN* SILK. THE EFFECT OF AN ABSTRACT AND BIZARRE PATTERN CAN BE SEEN. THE PATTERN HAS *GANGA-JAMUNI ZARI* WORK WHILE THE SILVER WORK IS DONE WITH *TASHI ZARI*.

been one of the reasons for the growth of the silk brocade industry in Varanasi in the eighteenth century, because 'the Shia world of Murshidabad and Lucknow was continually refreshed by immigrants from the cultural centres of Iran and Iraq.'[30]

The Persian-Islamic culture prevalent in the state of Awadh at that time (in which Varanasi was a major centre) encouraged the flow of Persian literature, art and artisans to the state. A group of Persian artists were also influenced by Indian aesthetics. Traders, always looking for new variations in pattern, took advantage of it. Illustrated Persian manuscripts and pattern books which had Persian and European designs were much in demand. Similarly, though the *asharfi buti* was a gold coin-shaped pattern, it is possible that it was made fashionable by a group of people in Awadh called Ashraf[31], who claimed that their ancestors came from outside the subcontinent, and were men of Arab, Iranian, Turkish or Afghan descent. They cherished everything they regarded as the Persian-Islamic culture - from their style of dressing, manners, architecture, painting, literature, sports, and amusement. Ashraf is also the name of a town in Persia, south of the Caspian Sea, which has a palace of Shah Abbas.

References

1. The Balkh mosque, known as *Masjid-i-Tarikh* (Mosque of History), is described by Lisa Golombek in her article *Abbasid Mosque at Balkh*, Oriental Art, Vol. XV, No. 3, p. 173, 1969. In the *Mahabharata,* the king of Balkh is said to have presented King Yudhisthira with beautiful textiles from his country when he came to participate in the *Rajasuya Yajna.*

2. A slave called Pishrukhan, a good tailor and dancer, was presented by Shah Tahmasp to Humayun. Akbar promoted him to the post of superintendent of the royal *farrash khana* (carpet department). He also served Jahangir during his reign. His death at the age of ninety and his tailoring skills were mentioned in Jahangir's memoirs, ample proof of his importance in the court.

3. *Rupam*, No. 33-34, January-April, 1928.

4. The Islamic book containing rules of conduct.

5. Hunting was the favourite sport of the Persian and Mughal rulers.

6. It is said that the depiction of young boys in Islamic art has a religious connotation. They are supposed to represent the *ghilmans* mentioned in the Quran (where the joys of paradise are described); and are depicted as heavenly attendants of the faithful, going about with goblets and cups overflowing with wine.

7. The Indian Heritage, *Court Life and Arts Under Mughal Rule,* catalogue, Victoria and Albert Museum, pp. 94-95.

8. A similarly patterned early nineteenth-century silver enamelled *farshi* (hookah base) in Bharat Kala Bhavan, Varanasi, is one of the finest representations of this motif in decorative arts.

9. Muqarrab Khan, the governor of the port of Cambay, where foreign goods were unloaded, sometimes sent unusual imported gifts to Jahangir. On the occasion of Jahangir's marriage to the daughter of Jagat Singh, he sent the Emperor a European tapestry which Jahangir found exceptionally beautiful.

10. A similarly patterned shawl in the Powis Collection in the UK is said to have been bought by Lord Clive in A.D. 1804.

11. Swietochowski, Marie C., *The Emperor's Album*, Metropolitan Museum of Art, New York, p. 45.

12. Welch, Stuart Cary, *The Art of Mughal India,* p. 67, New York, 1976.

13. Shahjahan receiving his three sons and Asaf Khan during his accession ceremony.

14. The storehouse of royal furnishings.

15. A painting (of a picnic party) from the Anwar-e-Suhail manuscript (A.D. 1580) in the Bharat Kala Bhavan collection shows seven figures wearing long gowns patterned with Chinese clouds. and golden flying and sitting birds - a Persian or Chinese motif. Fabrics with similar colours and motifs can be seen in paintings of the *Badshahnama* in furnishing material.

16. The floral motifs and geometrical designs used in the decoration of the Taj Mahal (A.D. 1648) were widely used in Mughal art. The architect of the Taj was a Central Asian person called Ahmed. He was given the title of *Nadir-ul-Asr* (Best of the Age) by Shahjahan. It is possible that he introduced the famous drooping floral plant motif to Mughal art, which became famous as the *latifa buta*.

17. In Kashmir, in A.D. 1667, another Shalimar Bagh was made in Lahore by Ali Mardan Khan, the celebrated engineer of the Mughal court.

18. The literal meaning is 'breaking the colour'. A similar technique was adopted in Kashmir for making shawls and *patkas*. (A fine example is seen in the Bharat Kala Bhavan collection.)

19. Welch, S.C., op. cit., p. 67.

20. Akbar held court at Lahore from A.D. 1584 to 1598, where he was visited by many European missionaries and envoys, including Fitch, Newbery, Leeds and Stomy.

21. The textile ateliers at Samarkand and Bukhara (Central Asia) were established by Timur in A.D. 1401. When he occupied Damascus, he deported many of its artisans (including weavers) to Samarkand, because Damascus was known for its superb metalware, arms and textiles.

22. The Magyar-sleeved jacket popularised by Jahangir.

23. Saracen was the general name among the Greeks and Romans for the nomads of Syro-Arabian descent, who were known for making and trading fine damask silk.

24. Dasgupta, R., *Art of Medieval Assam*, p. 200.

25. According to Major Walsh, in the late nineteenth century, a man's suit was available for three twelve rupees, and a handkerchief for one rupee.

26. *Chinoiserie* was a style based on Chinese designs, made fashionable after the opening of the Persian and Siamese embassies in Paris. All exotic patterns came to be called *Chinoiserie,* even if they were made in Persia, India or Mexico, and they were markedly different from the prevailing style.

27. Madame Pompadour, mistress of Louis XV, was known for introducing new fashions (in hairstyles, dresses, and so forth) among the elite in French society.

28. Introduced in France by Joseph Marie Jacquard, a mechanic born in Lyons in A.D. 1752.

29. Spitalfield, the brocade-weaving centre in England, stopped being a major silk- and damask-producing unit in A.D. 1824. Norwich produced patterned brocades of mixed fabric, i.e., silk and wool. These were popular in India in the nineteenth century, mainly as shawls and upholstery. The English floral patterns woven on them were copied by the brocade weavers of Varanasi.

30. Canfield, Robert L., ed, *Turko-Persian in Historical Perspective,* p. 117

31. Ibid., p. 105.

VARANASI: A SPECIAL REFERENCE

Few cities in the world can claim an unbroken tradition in spite of political and social changes. Banaras (Varanasi or Kashi) is one of them. Its textile industry shares its antiquity with the town. It has outwitted the vicissitudes of time and thrives till today.

It is amazing that some of the descriptions of the city in the third and fourth centuries B.C. more or less match those of modern Varanasi. At that time, it was considered one of the seven premier cities of India. The city had a moat around it and a surrounding wall with four main gates which were closed at night. Several localities and suburbs were allotted to people of different professions, and the habitation of the weavers and hunters were on the outskirts of the city.[1] It was a rich flourishing city and a great emporium of trade and industry, famous for different varieties of textiles, particularly its soft flimsy muslins, perfumes, ointments and ivory – which were traded to different parts of India by caravans which comprised as many as five hundred carts.[2] Ancient literary sources mention Kashi as an important weaving centre. According to Buddhist literature, fabrics made in Varanasi were pleasant to handle, beautiful to look at, and expensive and were greatly popular with rich and discerning people all over the country. Sanskrit and Jain literature also mention Kashi as an important weaving and trading centre. Specific types of fabrics can be linked to Kashi as is seen in their names such as *varanaseyyaka,*[3] *kasikuttam, kasikamsu* and *kasika.*[4] According to Patanjali, *kasika* textiles made during the Sunga period (second and first century B.C.) were more expensive and probably of better quality than similar material called *shatak* made in Mathura, which was also a textile weaving centre. This was a major item of trade of the city in the Kushan period (first to third centuries A.D.). *Shataka* was the male garment used either as a dhoti or *uttariya,* the upper scarf. Since a comparison was made between the two fabrics, it seems *kasika* was also a fine quality of dhoti or *dupatta* for which Varanasi was famous in later periods.

Damodar Gupta (late eighth century A.D.), in his work *Kuttanimattam,* while describing the glory of Varanasi, mentions a lower garment decorated with gold thread (*kanakagarbhita*), worn by the wealthy people in Kashi.[5] This may have been the *Kashika vastra* mentioned above. Plain fabrics with gold borders continued to be made even during the Mughal period, and till the early twentieth century.

Political disturbances from the eighth century till the establishment of the Mughal empire in A.D. 1526 must have affected, to

Preceding page 120

■ Plate: 106
BLOUSE, VARANASI, LATE
19TH OR EARLY 20TH
CENTURY. CLOSELY
ARRANGED GOLDEN *ZARI*,
SINGLE-FLOWER *BUTIS* IN AN
OVAL FORMAT (*BADAMA*).

an extent, the textile industry of Varanasi. The *Tarikh-us-Subuktigin,* written by Baihaqi in A.D. 1034, praises the Banaras textiles and lists them in the category as one of the most prized possessions among the booty won in the war. In A.D. 1394, Mohammad Shah Tughlak, the Sultan of Delhi, conferred the title of Malik-us-Sharq on Khwaja-i-Jahan, who carved out the independent kingdom of Jaunpur, including Varanasi which received political and economic attention under the Sharqi kings. His successor Ibrahim Shah Sharqi appointed Mohammasd Khalis as the Governor of Varanasi.[6] The area called Khalispura (near Madanpura), along the bank of the Ganga, was probably named after him and was known for its fine cotton textiles and *zari*-worked cotton fabrics. Later most of the weavers of this area shifted to Madanpura.

During Akbar's reign, Varanasi was famous for the manufacture of fabrics, particularly those called *jholi* (this may have been the *jhul* which was used to cover the elephant's back during a procession), and *mihirkul* (a kind of muslin), mentioned by Abul Fazl. In Shahjahan's time, Varanasi continued to be famous for the production of cummerbunds, turbans, and garments, particularly for women.[7] Women's garments can easily be identified as *odhnis* or *dupattas* (veils or long scarves), which were the speciality of Varanasi, even in the eighteenth and nineteenth centuries.

Ralph Finch[8] mentions Varanasi as a thriving cotton textile centre. He writes that gold or silver *zari* turbans were supplied to the Mughal court by Varanasi weavers. Tavernier,[9] who visited the city on December 12-13, 1665, described it as prosperous, mainly because of its textile industry. He noticed a caravansarai, where the weavers directly sold their textiles to customers.[10] The cotton and silk fabrics were exceptional. They were checked for their quality, and stamped with the imperial seal. If their quality was not up to the mark, the merchants were flogged. Nicolai Manucci, in his travel book, *Storia Do Mogor* (the late seventeenth century), records that the gold and silver fabrics of Varanasi were exported all over the world.

The Varanasi trade and economy experienced a temporary setback when its traders paid Ahmed Shah Bangash a fat ransom in A.D. 1750 to stop his advancing troops. The invasion of the Rohillas and the dispute between Raja Balwant Singh of Varanasi and the Nawab of Awadh further worsened the situation. Later, Varanasi was transferred to the British East India Company, and a period of political calm, so important for economic development, followed. Attracted by this, many exiled noblemen, Mughal princes, scions of the house of Awadh, Marathas of the Peshwa family, and pious upper-class Hindus began settling in Varanasi and enhanced the cultural and economic life of the city. The textile industry too reached its zenith. Many English travellers and important visitors, in the early nineteenth century, gave detailed accounts of the glory of Banaras textiles. Lord George Valentia[11] found them 'beautiful but very expensive and fit to be used on important occasions only.' The prosperity of the city largely depended on its textile industry, and fabrics were exported to

Europe too. Bishop Reginald Heber[12] described Varanasi as 'a great trade centre and a market for Kashmir shawls, Dacca muslin and its own manufactures.' Mrs Colin Mackenzie[13] travelled to Varanasi in A.D. 1847, and visited one of the richest manufacturers of Banaras brocade. She was amazed at the magnificence of the fabric and found it to be much superior in quality to European brocades. She also writes that 'some of the muslins spotted with gold, muslin shawls, and scarves with gold and silver borders, (*jamdari odhni*) [sold] for about thirty rupees, were beautiful.' Brocade was used for both men's and women's garments. She describes the fashions prevalent among people of high society and a prince wearing 'wide trousers'. During her visit to the Raja of Satna, she describes the dress worn by a royal lady as a 'very short red jacket with short sleeves' (made of cloth of gold), a red drapery (*odhni*) sprinkled or embroidered with gold, and stiff outstanding petticoats (*lehenga*) of red gold.'

Many Gujarati and Agrawal businessmen (*mahajans*) who settled in Varanasi in the late eighteenth or nineteenth century also gave a boost to the textile industry. Many Gujarati weavers and jewellers also migrated there, fleeing from natural calamities and political disturbances in their homeland and continued the business for which they were renowned. Another major factor which contributed to the boom was that the East India company shifted the trade centre from Gujarat to Bengal and elevated sericulture to an organised industry. Thus, the Banaras textile industry was given a fresh lease of life; and the highly developed skills of the weavers were utilised, with the investment and management skills of the traders. In these peaceful conditions the movement of raw material and finished goods was smooth. The Company encouraged the businessmen because it needed money, and took loans from them, giving them power and high posts.[14] Each community carved out its own locality. The Gujaratis who were mainly Vaishnavites, and followers of the Vallabha Sampradaya cult, settled mainly around the Gopal Mandir (temple) in Thatheri Bazar. The Agrawals too, were mainly Vaishnavites (though there were Jain traders also) and settled mainly around the centre of the town, such as Thatheri Bazar, Chowk, Kunj Gali, Raja Darwaja, Bulanala etc. Another old business community actively involved in the textile business and settled around these areas, were Khatris. The number of Punjabi businessmen grew after Partition in 1947. The textile business, however, still remains in the hands of the communities mentioned above.

The eclectic groups of people effected fashion trends and designs. Every social or religious group had its own norms regarding the colour, design or material of their garments, from the weavers who came after the fall of the Mughal Empire and disturbances in Awadh to the Gujarati, Marathi and Bengali settlers who came to Varanasi around the late eighteenth and nineteenth centuries.

During the Mughal period, the areas inhabited by weavers were between Madhorao Minar, Dhai Kangura Ki Masjid, Khalispura and Madanpura, near the riverfront, which provided the necessary humidity and water for the weaving of fine cotton fabrics. When the increasing population of weavers forced many of them to live farther away from the river to get the required humidity for weaving cotton, they would hang damp white cotton curtains on the doors and windows to keep out the sunlight and hot air, and also ensured that the floor (made of raw soil) remained moist. Originally these were mainly cotton weavers. But cotton gradually lost its importance with the introduction of silk (easily available from Bengal), which was easier to weave and more profitable than cotton. Also, other cotton *jamdani*-weaving centres such as Tanda and Dacca, produced better quality and probably less expensive fabrics.

The traditional pit-throw shuttle looms, mostly used by Varanasi weavers, have been handed down from father to son for generations. Certain improvements have, however, been made in the technique of weaving and in the tools used.

The old pit loom used to weave cotton had different scales for the number of warp and weft used in the weaving. The wide spacing between the threads had to be changed for weaving silk (which requires a more compact arrangement for a dense weave). The *gathwa* (heddle or thread-frame) system was introduced towards the end of the sixteenth century by Khwaja Abdul Samad Kashmiri[15] who came to Varanasi during Akbar's reign. He designed various types of *gathwas*(thread-frames) operated on looms which enabled the weavers to introduce various artistic and floral designs in the weaving process with ease and efficiency. Further improvements made

during the last three centuries brought about major innovations in the weaving of floral designs, borders and *pallus*.

Jacquard looms were introduced in Varanasi by the Alaipura weavers in the early 1930s and proved to be a boon for the silk industry. In spite of the troubled war years (1939-1945), the demand for Banaras goods was always in excess of the quantity produced. A variety of textures, designs and patterns were introduced, and a number of looms were installed, increasing production tremendously.

Independence in 1947 brought in its wake the partition of the subcontinent. Many weavers migrated to Pakistan. The silk-weaving industry in Varanasi had for centuries been divided between the Hindus and the Muslims. The Hindus monopolised trade, while the weavers were mostly Muslim. (Now the Muslims have also entered trading, but to a lesser extent.)

After Independence, India abolished the princely states and the *zamindari* system. This diminished the ranks of the feudal nobility who had been the main users of the rich textiles.[16] Once again the textile industry had to adapt itself to the changed circumstances. Cheaper saris and fabrics began to be made for the masses using cheap material and quick pattern weaving techniques like *fekwa*. The popularity of European clothes among Indian males also contributed to the recession in the industry. However, for weddings and other ceremonies, Banaras textiles were still de rigueur.

The revival of traditional patterns and techniques in 1982 was a turning point for the Banaras silk industry. The Festivals of

India organised in the UK, USA, Russia, France and other European countries again made Indians aware of and made them cherish their rich heritage. This fostered a demand for traditional patterns and techniques. Textile and fashion designers drew inspiration from old fabric pieces kept in museums. Even today *jamdanis, balucharis, himrus,* tissues and *kimkhwabs* are greatly valued.

TRADITIONAL WEAVING AREAS IN VARANASI

Alaipura and Madanpur are considered traditional weaving *mohallas* (areas) in Varanasi, and the weavers there continue to make their distinctive textiles. Each group has its own originality, which is easily distinguishable.

Madanpura

There are two theories of how the area acquired its name, both substantiating its antiquity and centuries-old weaving tradition. The first that it was named after the Gahadwal king Madanpal,[17] who ruled Varanasi from A.D. 1100-1114, and the second is that it was named after King Madan Verma of the Chandela dynasty, who received Varanasi in the form of a land grant.[18] Madanpura was also called Madanphoora[19] (the place of peace). It is said to have been protected by seven gates from the wild animals of the surrounding jungles. Perhaps the gates also protected weavers from the repeated attacks of invaders.

Documents[20] in the possession of some old weaving families of Varanasi yield valuable information about the development of the weaving industry. *Akhbarul Mokhadim* (1924), an unpublished book, mentions weaving as the main occupation of the Muslims. Its sources of information were several old documents, such as the *Ferman-i-Shahi,* the proclamations of emperors and judgments given in the courts during the Muslim and British periods. According to it, the first caravan of Muslims entered Varanasi in the eleventh century (380 Al Hizri). As their religion, appearance and dress were all different from that of the local Hindu population, they were asked to stay outside the main city. Madanpura at that time formed the city's southern border (and was surrounded by forests), and Alaipura the northern boundary.

The weavers who settled in Madanpura were a group of seven families, later called *sat gharua.*[21] They had fled from central Asia or the western Iranian plateau. According to the late Mohammad Ayub[22] of Madanpura, these seven families first settled around Delhi, before shifting to Varanasi. They may have belonged to a group of *kazzaz* weavers who had migrated from west Asian weaving centres, and were employed in the royal weaving workshops of the Sultanate kings. They were the descendents of Hazrat Sisalahi Salam, their patron saint, and settled in Madanpura within the limits of the seven gates.[23] Gradually this became a famous weaving centre in Varanasi. The fine cotton turban material and *patkas* with plain *zari* borders and ends were the speciality of Banaras weavers, for which they received the royal titles such as *chira-i-baff*[24] or 'the weavers of turbans' and *Noorbaff,*[25] the light of weavers or best of weavers. Such *patka*s, called *damani*, and turban material called *safa*, continued to be woven in Varanasi until the early twentieth century. In a portrait of Shahjahan in the Victoria and Albert Museum, London, the Emperor is shown wearing a similar plain gold-bordered white *patka* thrown around his shoulder and tied to his waist. According to Abdul Awwal (a weaver and textile designer in Varanasi), the *damani* was an important part of court dress and was also supplied to the royal courts of south India.

It is said that the weavers belonging to the seven families brought with them a special silk-weaving technique for *kazazi* and *nassaji* fabrics from Khujistan in the western plateau of Iran. The technique was called *urtu*.[26] It was woven with the *gathwa* loom in Varanasi. Therefore, the art of weaving Banaras brocades may be a continuation of the techniques and designs used in the ancient centres of Baghdad, Susa, Ur, and other places. (*Khazz* and *nassij* brocades were woven at Baghdad, Kufa Basra, Fars and other weaving centres.)

According to Dr Mohammad Zahir, before the Muslims dominated the weaving industry, it was the monopoly of a 'sub-caste of Khatri Hindus known as Pattikas'. These Pattikas (or *Pattakars*) helped the migrant Muslim weavers establish their craft, maybe by providing them with funds and raw materials. The finished products made by the Muslim weavers were marketed by the Khatris,[27] because the newly-settled Muslims were not allowed to have any direct contact with high-caste Hindus. This proved to be a profitable arrangement. The Muslim

weavers were skilled and their labour cheap because they had to accept whatever they were paid to establish themselves. Their beneficiaries, the Khatris, began concentrating more on marketing. Thus weaving passed into the hands of the Muslims, while the Khatri Hindus became traders. (Among the Muslim weavers, there are some whose ancestors had migrated to Varanasi; the others are mostly the progeny of converts to Islam, who changed their religion to escape persecution by the Muslim rulers.)

According to some old families of the area, the Madanpura community of weavers were Persian- and Turkish-speaking. Their extremely fine workmanship made them exclusive, and till a few years ago they regarded themselves as superior to the weavers of other localities (particularly those of Alaipura and Badi Bazar). Madanpura weavers were renowned for producing a lightweight and fine silk gauze material called s*uti Banarasi*, with cotton warp and silk weft, and patterns woven with gold and silver thread. Fine golden borders, *butis* and *pallus* were the speciality of Banarasi saris, *dupattas* (Plate 107) and yardage material, which were noted for their highly sophisticated designs and colours (Plates 4, 10, 10a; pages 17, 27). A typical Banarasi *dupatta* pattern was an adaptation of the square Kashimiri shawl and was called *purmatan dupatta*. It had four *konia* (stylised mango forms) at the corners, plain *zari* panels and borders, the ground was filled either with diagonal creepers (*ari jhari*) or floral *butis*. There was a big round medallion in the centre (Plate 93; page 108). The Madanpura weavers also made fabrics

Facing Page

■ Plate: 107
ODHNI, VARANASI, 19TH CENTURY. THIS EXAMPLE OF *RANGKAT* TECHNIQUE HAS A TWO-COLOUR GROUND; THE PATTERN IS THE USUAL *ARI JHARI*; *CARRIE, KONIA,* AND A BROAD PLAIN GOLD *CHAUDANI PALLU* OUTLINE BY *MOTHRA*.

for the royal states of Varanasi, Hyderabad, Lucknow, Rampur, Jamnagar, Junagarh among others.

Weaving with the *gathwa* loom was a speciality of the Madanpura weavers, who produced a variety of patterns to cover the background. *Khaskhasi, laharia, chaudani, khajuri, konia* and *chand* are a few well-known examples.

Nal pherwa, or the three-shuttle technique, was used in Varanasi and Chanderi, and in saris from south India. This was the traditional Indian weave, in which two weft shuttles were used for weaving contrast borders and one for the ground.

The selvedges of the fabrics made in Madanpura were neat compared to those woven in Alaipura; the *kshir* or endings of the *pallu* were more compact and thinner, and the golden lines were closer to each other. The selvedges of Alaipura fabrics were rather rough and uneven, and the gap between the *kshir* was wider too.

Alaipura

Another weaving locality known for its distinct style is situated on the northern boundary of old Banaras and is Alaipura or Alvipura.[28]

The weaving areas around Alaipura are Badi Bazar, Pilikothi, Kacchi Bara, Katehar, Tartale, Raja Pura, Dulli Derhi, Mohammad Shahid, Ambia Mandi, Hanuman Phatak, Chittanpura, Pathani Tola, Omkareshwar, Koyla Bazar, Jalalipatti, Doshipura, Bakaria Kund etc. These areas have their histories too. The *dargah* (tomb) of Fakhruddin Alvi perhaps gave the name Alvi Pura which was later distorted to Alaipura. Doshipura had a structure with thirty-two columns, which was a Buddhist monastery according to some local weavers. The weavers of Doshipura are said to belong to the *Panch Gharwa* or five families, believed to be Rajputs, the Hindu warrior caste[29], who later converted to Shia Muslims. The customs which prevailed here, (till the late 1970s) were an amalgamation of Hindu and Muslim cultures. During a marriage ceremony, the Muslim *Nikah* was followed by the Hindu *Saptapadi*. The Hindu God, Shri Satyanarayana (Lord Vishnu) was worshipped too and was called *Satyapir*.[30]

Most of the weavers who settled in Badi Bazar, Pilikothi and Jaitpura had migrated to Varanasi from Mau, Aima (near Allahabad) and Man Nath Bhanjan (near Azamgarh) and nearby areas. The weavers of Alaipura are generally called *mauwals*; they follow the tradition of Ayub Ansari, and pray to him before starting any new work. They claim their ancestors came from Turkey, Persia or central Asian countries, which could be true, because the type of fabrics they produce, their technique, and so forth, were similar to that of those countries. They may also be the descendents of weavers who had been employed in the royal workshops of Lahore, Agra, Delhi, and and other places, who migrated to Varanasi after the disintegration of the Mughal Empire.

It is said that Sher Shah (A.D. 1540-1545) visited the renowned Sufi mystic, Said Ahmad Badhwa, who lived in a *dargah* near Mau, twice. Later, two Mughal princesses, Jahan Ara and Chaman Ara, daughters of Emperor Shahjahan, visited the *dargah* in Mau. They had a *shahi* (royal) mosque and quarters for soldiers constructed, and named the place Jahanabad, which is in Azamgarh district. It is said that craftsmen, particularly weavers, were brought from Agra (most probably from royal Mughal workshops) to settle there, perhaps to produce ceremonial fabric for the *dargah* and the mosque. Mau was connected with the Grand Trunk Road by a bridge across the Tons River (broken during the floods of 1955), which facilitated communication and trade. The above mentioned *mauwals* of Alaipura probably belonged to this community of weavers.

If Madanpura weavers were known for their fine and delicate traditional work on *kinkhab*, Alaipura weavers were renowned for experimenting with new techniques and designs and implementing innovations which became necessary as they had to compete with the well-settled traditional weavers of Madanpura, who already excelled in their craft. Thick and heavy *zari* and silk fabrics, mainly used as furnishing and dress material using twill and satin weave, were made by them. Even though their compact weaving technique required more raw material and was much more laborious as the weft had to be pressed harder with no gaps, their fabrics were cheaper than those of Madanpura. *Galta* and *sangi,* and heavy silk brocade yardages such as *Arabi than* and *gyasar* (Chinese ceremonial brocade) were made here, and became a speciality of the area. These fabrics could not be copied by Madanpura weavers because they required too much labour on the loom. They had originally been the weavers of lighter fabric (cotton) who later switched to silk. Hence, the lightness and delicacy of their work was maintained in the silk fabrics they wove.

Satin weave was used to make *tanchui* saris and dress materials. Damask weaving was referred to as 'Vasket weaving' locally because these self-patterned satins were mainly used to make European style short waist coats called 'vasket' locally.

Mekhalas or *rehas* were made for the Assamese market. A local weaver called Gada Hussain was known for weaving them around 1930 to 1940. A weaver called Nazmu was famous for weaving *dupattas* called *pattakam*, with a width of 72 inches, for Gujarati and Marwari bridal costumes. It was a thick material made with *pat* weft (untwisted silk); and the *zal* was woven with *zari kalabattu.*

Experiments at Badi Bazar to produce copies of *paithanis, balucharis,* Kashmiri shawls and *ashavalis* achieved a reasonable success, and it came to be known as a centre for these fabrics. In fact, the credit of keeping the brocade industry alive even in its darkest hour goes to the weavers of Alaipura, who learned to adopt new techniques, and kept abreast with the changing fashions. Satin weave and the jacquard loom were used first in this. Two remarkable examples were the revival of *baluchari* saris by Kallu Hafiz, and the imitation of Chinese ceremonial brocade *gyasar* by Hazi Moinuddin of Pilikothi in 1940. Woollen and mixed woollen and silk shawls and dress materials are made here too. The yarn is mostly obtained from Punjab. The shawls usually have the *jamawar* pattern of Kashmir shawls. The replicas of large nineteenth century *jamawar* shawls are made here in pure silk.

Besides these weaving areas, the production centres in and around Varanasi

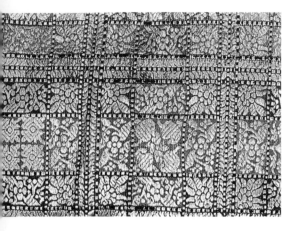  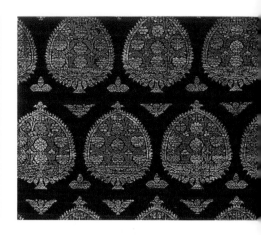

From left to right

■ Plate: 108
ANGARAKHA, VARANASI, EARLY
20TH CENTURY. A PATTERN
OF VARIEGATED *BUTAS* OF
GANGA-JAMUNI ZARI ARE
PLACED WITHIN MULTI-
COLOURED SQUARES.

■ Plate: 109
JACKET, VARANASI, LATE 19TH
CENTURY. THE *GANGA JAMUNI
ZARI* FLORAL *ZAL* PATTERN
DEPICTED ON A DEEP PINK
GROUND.

■ Plate: 110
LADIES' SKIRT, VARANASI,
19TH CENTURY. ROWS OF
GANGA-JAMUNI ZARI AND SILK
MINAKARI WORK WITH
FLOWERING PLANT MOTIFS
IN A BETEL LEAF FORMAT OR
PAN BUTA.

district are Nati Imli, Lallapura, Philkhana, Chittanpuru, Ramnagar, Lohta, Chiraigaon, Baburi, Baragaon, Ashapur and others. A few towns around Varanasi, such as Chunar, Chakia, Mirzapur, Azamgarh, Mau and some villages up to the border of Bihar, are also making copies of Banaras fabrics and supplying to Banaras traders.

DESIGN

Every social or religious group had its own norms regarding the colour, design and material of their garments. Mostly *mashru* or the mixed fabric was used by Muslims; *matka* silk by Hindus who also liked bright colours like red, yellow and orange. Muslims liked *kasni* (lavender), *uda* (sky blue), green, white, magenta, black, and so forth. The animal or human figured pattern was not favoured by the Muslims.

The natural forms are woven in a highly decorative and stylised manner. After assimilating the essence of a pattern, the designer implements his own interpretation of it. Thus, a leaf can evolve into a flower or a bird form. Decorative motifs like a leaf, flower, fruit, creeper, bird or animal never break the symmetry of the pattern.

Banaras weavers always gave serious consideration to the proper utilisation of the space between patterns. To maintain harmony and correlation between motifs, certain geometrical patterns were used – the most common being *khanjari* (chevron), *charkhana* (checks), *ari doria* (straight or diagonal lines), *mothra* (a double line containing a simple or running pattern inside), and so forth. *Mothra* is mainly used as a border, or to mark the division between different portions of a complex pattern. The floral forms are called *buti* or *buta*, according to their size. The *buti* is a single flower or figure made individually (Plates 106, 113; pages 120, 131). Different forms and flowers give their names to these *butas*. Some popular examples are *pan* (betel), *fardi* (the effect is produced by dots), *carrie* (mango), *tara* (star), *ashrafi* (circular, coin-shaped), and so forth. The *butis,* which are given the names of flowers, are called *phul* (flower) *butis,* such as *chameli* (jasmine), *champa, guldaudi* (chrysanthemum), *genda* (marigold), *gulab* (rose), and *parijat*. The number of petals used in a *buti* also give it its name, like *tinpatia* (three-petalled), *panchpatia* (five-petalled), *satpatia* (seven- petalled). If these *butis* are woven in a *bel* (creeper pattern), it is called *genda bel, guldaudi bel, gulab bel,* and so forth.

When the top pointed end of a *carrie* is turned around and further decorated, it is called a *kalgha buta* (Plate 115, page 133). A further embellishment of the pattern is to enclose a *buti* in a network of geometrical patterns called *jal* or trellis (Plates 103, 116; pages 115, 133). Another outstanding example of *Banarsi Jal* has the intermingling floral creepers or patterns covering the entire ground (Plates 109, 111; pages 130, 131). This is also called the *Banarsi Hunar.*

Textile designs inspired by foreign patterns were adapted in such a way that they lost their alien nature. For example, the Persian *shikargah* (hunting scene) pattern using trees, creepers, flowers, birds, animals, and even human figures became a specialty of Varanasi in the late nineteenth century

(plates 85, 95; pages 102, 110). Sometimes, more than one foreign motif and design was incorporated in a single piece of fabric so cleverly that they blended effortlessly with the essentially Indian pattern. Very common examples are carrie and *latifa buti* of Persian origin (Plates 14, 86; pages 32, 103), the Arabian *mehrab* or Turkish ogival trellis (Plates 103, 116; pages 115, 133) and so forth.

Inscriptions either religious or secular were a popular form of decoration in art, such as the Hispano-Arabic, 'Long life to our Honourable Sultan'. In European fabrics too, religious inscriptions, mostly in Latin, were woven on the robes of religious leaders, and *Orphreg web,* a narrow cloth of gold with religious inscriptions was produced in large quantities in Cologne, Venice, and Florence.

Decorative inscriptions were popular in Banares too and the weavers made such fabrics which were very much in fashion till the early twentieth century. Shamshuddin of Pilkothi and Jagannath of Ramnagar wove such patterns. These were mostly commissioned by rich patrons. 'Long live Shri Pradyumna Singh Ji Saheb' (in English)

From left to right

■ Plate: 111
YARDAGE, VARANASI, 19TH CENTURY. CLOSELY ARRANGED *GULDWADI* (CRYSANTHEMUM) *BUTIS* FORM A *JAL* ON YELLOW SATIN GROUND. THE *BUTIS* ARE WOVEN IN SILVER *ZARI* AND OUTLINED WITH SILK.

■ Plate: 112
PYJAMA, EARLY 20T CENTURY, VARANASI, ZOOMORPHIC PATTERN. THE PEACOCK FORM IS TURNED CLEVERLY INTO STYLISED MARIGOLD FLOWER *BUTI*.

■ Plate: 113
JACKET, 19TH CENTURY. CLOSELY ARRANGED ROWS OF ROSE *BUTIS* IN GOLDEN *ZARI* ON RED. THE *BUTIS* HAVE A BUD ON TOP OF THE FLOWER PROJECTING TOWARDS THE LEFT, BREAKING THE OVAL FORMAT.

was woven alongside a deer design inside *chand butis* (roundels). This fabric was made in 1938 for the king of Rajkot. *Pati Seva Stri Dharma* (a woman's religion is to serve her husband), and *Agar Bhagwan Har Sthan Par to Achuta Kaun?* (If God is everywhere who is untouchable?), were woven on a sari (in Devanagari script) for the Maharani of Baroda in the 1940s. *Dupattas* with religious invocations and the names of deities, such as *Ram Ram* and *Om Namah Shivaya*, were popular with the Hindus. Those with the former name are called *Ramnami dupattas* (Plate 121) and are still very popular in Varanasi. Block-printed *chadars* were made in Murshidabad district with such religious insriptions. Religious inscriptions on fabrics, in Persian and Arabic, such as *Bismillah-Hir-Rahman-E-Rahim*, or other verses from the Quran, were popular and exported to the Middle East.

Two famous Banaras designers, Tajammul Hussain and Mohammad Hussain, participated in a London exhibition of Indian handicrafts in 1895. They brought back with them a new pattern book, which mainly had English wallpaper and French and English velvet patterns – these they incorporated into Banaras brocade designs (Plates 97, 98; page 111). English flowers, foliage, pomegranates, heraldic patterns, architecture, vase patterns, French net patterns, and so forth, were popular in pre-independent India. Borders, or creepers were no longer bounded on either side by the traditional narrow *bel*, but were left free. *Konia* almost disappeared or became only symbolic (Plate 105; page 116). The effect of light and shade (*dhup chawn*) was also introduced in textiles by using light and dark shades of yarns of the same colour, similar to the *point rentre* technique used by French weavers. Light-textured fabrics were preferred. A sari called *suggi ki sari* was very much in fashion till 1950. Woven on the *gathwa* loom, it was as light as a bird, hence the name *sugga* (parrot). The design could also have given the fabric its name.

In 1942-45, a specially designed textile, *Arabi than*, was woven for export to the Middle East. It had a special pattern of big *khazur* (date) trees, and other large floral and star patterns. *Gyasar* (a copy of ceremonial Chinese brocade) used in Buddhist monasteries and for Buddhist religious symbols, such as dragons and stylised clouds, form the main patterns. Some Japanese motifs were also used.

The period after Indian Independence (1947-65) was a dark phase for the Banaras textile industry. Many Muslim weavers had migrated to Pakistan. The princely states and the aristocracy were on the decline. Also, the fashion of the time demanded a simpler and more practical dress code. There was a decrease in the demand for traditional dresses and the material used in making them. Interest in evolving new patterns almost vanished, and those that were used lacked their former originality and beauty.

The Vishwakarma Exhibitions (Festivals of India), held in the UK, France and the USA between 1982-85, proved to be the catalyst which revived traditional Indian patterns and fabrics. Copies of traditional designs, preserved in museums and private collections, were made for the exhibition and became a great success with the fashion

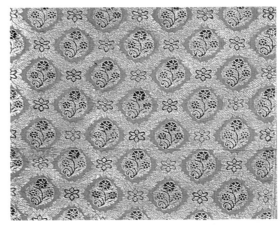

Facing page

■ Plate: 114
SARI, DETAIL, VARANASI, EARLY 20TH CENTURY. DEEP PURPLE SILK GROUND PATTERNED WITH GOLD *ZARI* SUCH AS CARRIE ENCLOSING THE SHIKARGAH PATTERN, AN UNDULATING CHRYSANTHEMUM CREEPER CALLED *GOZAR BEL* AND A COMPOSITE CARRIE PATTERN ARE AT THE CORNER. A TOUCH OF WESTERN INFLUENCE LIES IN THE FLORAL *JAL* PATTERN OF THE GROUND.

From top to bottom

■ Plate: 115
LADIES' BLOUSE, VARANASI, EARLY 20TH CENTURY. SILK GROUND OVER WHICH CLOSELY ARRANGED *CARRIE BUTIS* OF GOLD *ZARI* ARE FINELY WORKED.

■ Plate: 116
YARDAGE, VARANASI (ALAIPURA), EARLY 20TH CENTURY. THE GROUND HAS SMALL *MINAKARI* AND SILVER *ZARI BUTIS* WITHIN A SILVER *BADRUM ZAL* - THE DESIGN IS CALLED *PATTA ZAL*.

■ Plate: 117
BROCADE FRAGMENT, 19TH CENTURY, VARANASI. GOLDEN *BUTIS* ON SATIN GROUND; THE *BUTIS* ARE THE SYNTHEIS OF PAN AND *CARRIE BUTA*.

133

nakshabandi cult of central Asia, often mentioned in Mughal chronicles. It is believed that the art was introduced in Bukhara in the fourteenth century by a Sufi saint, Khwaja Bahauddin. To him young *nakshabandis*, after their training under a master or *ustad*, offer prayers from their first income. Ghiyas-ud-din Nakshaband, mentioned in the *Ain-i-Akbari*, was a celebrated weaver in Akbar's royal workshop. Fabrics woven by him were highly priced and used only by the royalty. The *nakshabands* make patterns on small wooden frames with cotton thread. This woven pattern, called *jala*, is then hung on the loom and its threads attached to the pattern weft of the fabric. Some well-known *nakshabands* of Varanasi were Mohammad Hussain, Tajammul Hussain, Zafar Ustad, Fatul Ustad, Kallu Hafiz, Hazi Moinuddin, Hazi Abul Husan, Hafiz Shamiulla, Mohammad Yusuf and Mohammad Shamshudua.

Alaipura (Badi Bazar) is known for many illustrious weavers and *nakshabands*. Since the weavers here were more open to new ideas and innovations, they could copy any pattern. The copy invariably looked better than the original because of the innovations to the pattern that gave it a Banarasi touch.

Mohammad Hussain lived in Doshipura and was the disciple of Madhar, a renowned *nakshaband* of Alaipura in the nineteenth century. The *kinkhab* pieces made by him were selected for the Empire of India Exhibition held in London in 1895 and he was awarded there for his work.

Some of the other known *nakshabands* of the nineteenth century were Keeman Mia and Abdulla (who used to draw patterns on mica) of Kamalpura, Ishaq Mia of Rajapura, Anilulhuda, Shami Mia (also known for his cotton work) Hayatulla, Matiulla (alias Matuli Baba) and Khudabaksh of Doshipura. Hayatulla was famous for his patterns like *latifa buti, bela buti* and *chand buti*. He also wove a portrait of Queen Victoria with silk and *zari* for which he received a certificate of merit from the British government. His disciples were Matiulla and Khudabaksh; the latter's son, Rahmatulla, and grandsons Sakhawat Ali and Sajjad Ali were the famous *nakshabands* of the early twentieth century. Sajjad Ali's grandson, Muktar Hussain is a diploma holder in handloom technology and is a renowned weaver and designer. He introduced a new twill weave which brought depth and the effect of light and shade to a pattern. He calls it *Japani Urtu*.

Zafar Mia alias Zafar Ustad of Badi Bazar was a master weaver and *nakshaband* of the early twentieth century. He invented a pattern making technique called *pinjara* or cage. (According to Muktar Hussain, it was a sort of primitive Dobi loom, made of wood, still used in Chanderi.) The pattern making threads attached with a yoyo-like structure (called *chakwa* locally) were hung on the warp threads. It is said that if a pattern made by Zafar Mia was not liked by the client he used to modify it without erasing a single line.

Zafar Ustad's nephew, Hazi Abul Hasan alias Abu Sardar's (Kachchi Bag) family was known for weaving *sangi* and *galta* fabrics. His grandfather, Jamal, who migrated from Mau in the beginning of the nineteenth century was an expert weaver of *sangi* and

Facing page

■ Plate: 121
RAMNAMI DUPATTA, 19TH CENTURY, VARANASI/ GUJARAT. THE GROUND IS DIVIDED INTO SQUARES AND EACH SQUARE IS FILLED WITH THE NAME OF GOD RAMA IN DEVANAGARI. THE PAIR OF FEET USED AS THE PANEL MOTIF IS THE SYMBOLIC REPRESENTATION OF RAMA.

Bibliography

Aditi - The Living Arts of India, Catalogue of the Smithsonian Institution, USA.

Agrawal, V.S., *Kadambari*.

Agrawal, V.S., *Harsha Charita*.

Ahivasi, D., *Range Evem Chape Vastra*.

Alakajee Roshan, *Ancient Costumes*.

Anavian, R. & Ananion, G., *Royal Persian and Kashmir Brocades*.

Art of India, 1550-1990, Catalogue, Victoria & Albert Museum.

Asthana Shashi, *History and Archaeology of India's contacts with other Countries*.

Auberwile Dupont, *Classic Textile Design*.

Bagchi, P.C., *India and Central Asia*.

Bagchi, P.C., *India and China*.

Banerjee, J.N. , *Development of Hindu Iconography*.

Beach, C. Milo and Koch Ebba, *King of the World (The Padshahnama*.

Blochmann, H., *Ain-E-Akbari*, English trans.

Buch, M.A., *Economic Life in Ancient India*.

Buss Chira, *Silk Gold and Silver, 18th century textile*.

Berenier, F., *Travels in Mogul Empire*.

Canfield, R.L., ed., *Turko-Persia in Historical Perspective*.

Codrington, K. Deb, *Culture of Medieval India as illustrated in the Ajanta Frescoes*.

Daniel Defo, 'The Complete English Tradesman'.

Das, S.K., *Economic History of Ancient India*.

Dasgupta, A., *India and the Indian Ocean 1500-1800*.

Dasgupta, A., *Indian Merchants and the Decline of Surat, C. 1700-1750*.

Davar, F.C., *India and Iran Through the Ages*.

Desai, V., *Life at Court: Art of India's rulers, 16th-19th centuries*.

Dewar, F., *Silk Fabric of the Central Provinces*.

Dhamija Jasleen, ed., *Woven Silk of India*.

Doshi, S., ed., *Symbols of Manifestations of Indian Art*.

Du, Bois Emily, 'Banaras Brocade', *Ars Textrina, Encyclopedia of Art*.

Dwevedi, Dr Kapil Dev, *Sanskrit Vyakarana Evam Laghu Siddhant Kaumudi*.

Gelfer, A., *A History of Textile Art*.

Gentile, M., *Memories Sur I' Indoustan an Empire Mogal*.

Geoghegan, J, *Some Account of Silk in India*, Anthropology Design Series.

Ghosh, A., ed., *Ajanta Murals*.

Gillow, J., *Traditional Indian Textiles*.

Glacier, R., *Historic Textile Fabrics*.

Gopal Chandra, 'Old Forms and New Functions,' *Art in Industry*.

Goswami, B.N., ed., *Indian Painting*, Karl J. Khandalwala Felicitation Volume.

Goswami, B.N., *Essence of Indian Art*.

Gulati, A.N., *The Patolu of Gujarat*.

Gupta, B.A., *Thana Silks*, Journal of Indian Art.

Gupta, S.P., *Costumes, Textile, Cosmetics Coiffure in Ancient India*.

Hante, N.B., and Ponting, K.G., eds., *Cloth and Clothing in Medieval Europe*.

Hardiman, J.P., *Silk in Burma*, Journal of Indian Art and Industry.

Hennessy, E.B., *A History of Technology of Invention — Progress Through The Ages*, Vol. 1.

Imperial Gazetteers of India, 10 volumes.

Indian Art and Letters, Vol. 10.

Irwin John and Hall Margaret, *Indian Painted and Printed Fabrics*.

Irwin John, *Studies in Indian Textile History*.

Irwin John, Sarabhai Gira, Jayakar Pupul, eds., *Journal of Indian Textiles History*, Museum of Textiles, Ahmedabad, No. 1 to No. 7.

Jain, P.C., *Labour in Ancient India*.

Jain Rahul, *Minakari*, Catalogue on Mughal Patka.

Kashyap, J., *Dighanikaya*.

King Monique and King Donal, *European Textiles in the Kiev Collection 400 B.C. to A.D. 1800*.

Kinkhab, Journal of Indian Art, Vol. 1.

Kumar Tushar, *Saris of India*.

Le Motif Floral Dons Les Tissue Moghals.

Lentz, T.W. and Lawry, G.D., *Timur and the Princely Vision*.

Levin Bongard, *Studies in Ancient Indian and Central Asia.*

Liu Xinru, *Silk and Religion.*

Macdonnel, A and Keith B., *Vedic Index* (Hindi trans. Ramkumar Rai).

Majumdar, R.C., *Hindu Colonies in Far East Asia.*

Majumdar, R.C., *Corporate Life in Ancient India.*

Marg, Vol. 40, Nos. 1-4.

Marg , Vol. 34, Nos. 1-4.

Mathew, K.S., *Studies in Maritime History.*

Miller, B.S., *Gitagovinda* of Jayadeva.

Monnas, L. and Grangov, H., *Ancient and Medieval Textiles*, Studies in Honour of Donald King.

Mookerjee Ajit, ed., *Banaras Brocade.*

Mookerji, Gopal Nitya, *The Silk Industries of Bengal,* Journal of Indian Art.

Moti Chandra, *History of Indian costume from 1st-4th century A.D.,* Journal of Indian Society of Oriental Art, Calcutta, Vol 8.

Moti Chandra: *Kashi Ka Itihas* (Hindi).

Moti Chandra: *Costumes, Textiles, Cosmetics and Coiffure in Ancient and Medieval India.*

Moti Chandra: *Prachin Bhartiya Vesh Bhusha* (Hindi).

Munilal, *Mughal Harems.*

Murphy Veronica, *Europeans and the Textile Trade.*

Manucci, N., *Storia do Mogor.*

Nagari Pracharini Patrika, Part VIII and Part IX.

Oriental Art, Vol. 15.

'Origin of the Oriental Style in English Decorative Art', Burlington magazine, Vol. 97.

Pal, P., *Indian Paintings.*

Pal, P., ed., *Master Artists of The Imperial Mughal Court.*

Panikkar, K.M., *India and China.*

Pearson, M.N., *Merchants and Rulers in Gujarat*: *The Response to the Portuguese in the 16th Cent.*

Prasad Ishwari, *History of Medieval India.*

Prasad, Prakash Chandra, *Foreign Trade and Commerce in Ancient India.*

Rahim, A., *Mughal Relations with Central Asia.*

Rai Anand Krishna and Vijay Krishna, *Banaras Brocade.*

Rao, Gopinath T.A.G., *Elements of Hindu Icongraphy.*

Rawlinson, H.G., *Intercourse between India and the Western World.*

Reid, Anthony, *South East Asia in the Age of Commerce 1450-1680,* Vol. 2.

Riboud Krishna, ed., *In Quest of Themes and Skills,* Asian Textiles.

Riboud Krishna, ed., *Samit & Lampas – Indian Motifs.*

Riyaz-ul Islam, *The Relations between Mughal Emperors of India and Safavid Shahs* (unpublished Cambridge Ph.D. dessertation).

Roger Alexander and Bekeridge Henry, *Tuzuk-i-Jahangir.*

Rothamund Dietmar, *An Economic History of India.*

Rupam, (Journal) No. 4, October 1920.

Rupam, (Journal) No. 11, July 1922.

Rupam, (Journal) No. 33-34, January-April 1928.

Salmon, L., and Carlano, M., ed., *French Textiles: From Middle Ages Through The Second Empire.*

Sanskritiyana Rahul and Kashyap Jagdish, *Deegh Nikaya.*

Scott Phillappa, *The Book of Silk.*

Shamassastry, R., *Kautilya Arthshastra.*

Sharma, R.S., *Perspectives in Social and Economic History of Early India.*

Silk Fabrics of Bombay Presidency, Journal of Indian Art and Industry, Vol. 10.

Silk Fabrics of the Central Provinces, Journal of Indian Art, Vol. X.

Silk Industry in Punjab, Journal of Indian Art and Industry, Vol. 10.

Singh Chandramani, *A Catalogue – Textile and Constumes,* M.S. Man Singh Museum.

Singh Kiran, *Textile in Ancient India.*

Singhal, D.P., *India and the World Civilisation.*

Sir Leigh Ashton, ed., *Indian Textiles*, Catalogue of the exhibition held at the Royal Academy of Arts, London.

Sir Stein Aurel, *An Analysis of the Central Asian Silks*, South Western Journal of Anthropology, Vol. 1.

Sir Stein Aurel, *Ancient Khotan,* 2 Vol.

Sir Stein Aurel, *On Ancient Central Asian Tracks.*

Slomann Withel, *Bizarre Designs in Silks.*

Smith, V.A, *Early History of India.*

Steel, F.A., *Monograph on silk industry in the Punjab 1885-86.*

Sukul, K.N., *Varanasi Down the Ages.*

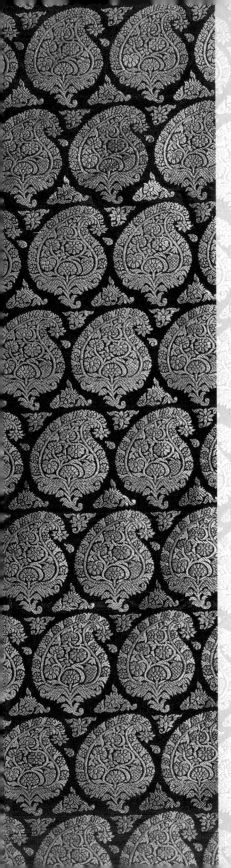

Tarn, W.W., *Greeks in Bactria and India.*

Tavernier, Jean-Bapist, *Travels in India.*

Textile Industry in Ancient India, Journal, Bihar and Orissa Research Society.

The Indian Heritage, Catalogue, Victoria & Albert Museum.

The Indian Antiquary, Vol. LIX.

The Indian Magazine, Vol. 7.

Treasures of Indian Textiles, Calico Museum.

Trivedi, A.B., *The Silk Weaving Industry of Surat,* Vol. X.

Tull Walch Major, J.H., *The History of Murshidabad.*

Weibel, A.C., *Two Thousand Years of Textiles,* Published for the Detroit Institute of Arts.

Upadhayay Baldev, *Sanskrit Sahitya Ka Itihas.*

Watson, F., *Advanced Textile Design.*

Watson, Forbes J., *The Textile Manufactures and the Costumes of the People of India.*

Watt George, *Indian Art at Delhi.*

Weibel A.C., *Indian Textiles.*

Welch Stuart, Cary, *The Art of Mughal India.*

Wilkinson, J.V.S., *Light of Canopus.*

Yusuf Ali, A., *Monograph on Silk Fabrics.*

Zimmer, H., *Myths and Symbolism of Indian Art.*